REALITY 101

REALITY 101

What It's Really Like to
Be a Teacher . . . And Teach, Too

Milton E. Rosenthal

A SCARECROWEDUCATION BOOK

The Scarecrow Press, Inc.
Lanham, Maryland, and Oxford
2003

A SCARECROWEDUCATION BOOK

Published in the United States of America
by Scarecrow Press, Inc.
A Member of the Rowman & Littlefield Publishing Group
4720 Boston Way, Lanham, Maryland 20706
www.scarecrowpress.com

PO Box 317
Oxford
OX2 9RU, UK

British Library Cataloguing in Publication Information Available

Library of Congress Cataloging-in-Publication Data
Rosenthal, Milton E., 1933–
  Reality 101 : what it's really like to be a teacher—and teach too / Milton E.
Rosenthal.
    p. cm.
"A ScarecrowEducation book."
  Includes bibliographical references (p.   ).
  ISBN 0-8108-4494-X (alk. paper)—ISBN 0-8108-4495-8 (pbk. : alk. paper)
  1. Teachers—United States. 2. Teaching—United States. I. Title.
LB1775.2 .R69 2003
371.1—dc21

                                                              2002030288

⊗™ The paper used in this publication meets the minimum requirements of
American National Standard for Information Sciences—Permanence of Paper
for Printed Library Materials, ANSI/NISO Z39.48-1992.
Manufactured in the United States of America.

To my late parents, my wife, my children, and grandchildren

To all future and current teachers, who *will* make a difference . . . and *do* make a difference in the lives of students

Teaching is not a lost art, but the regard for it is a lost tradition.

—Jacques Barzon

If you want to teach, put your heart and soul to the test and your fire, your energy, and your enthusiasm will transfer to your students.

—Milton Rosenthal

CONTENTS

PART 2 "WITHIN" THE PLANT

ACKNOWLEDGMENTS

I am fortunate to have worked and lived my life teaching. I have also been blessed with the opportunity to work with preteens, teenagers, young adults, and adults.

Words could never express my gratitude to my family who lived with my up days as well as my down days.

Specifically, my wife, Willa, who was (and continues to be) the sounding board as I related my daily experiences. Her ever-present support, patience, and loving kindness have enabled me to fulfill my life's ambitions.

My children, Jamie and Matthew, to some extent, lived the life of this teacher as well. They had no choice but to listen (and continue to listen) to some of my repetitive "stories." Matthew, who is currently teaching, continues to keep much of my writing in perspective. His evaluations and comments are priceless. His prowess with the computer is indispensable, and I relied on his expertise in compiling these materials.

I also wish to thank the many people whose "routine" conversations with me during my career allowed me to articulate my ideas and thoughts.

Thanks to Cindy Tursman for her assistance with the manuscript preparation guidelines and for her pertinent suggestions. Thanks to Amos Guinan for keeping me abreast of the publishing process and for addressing my concerns. Much appreciation to Thomas Koerner for extending to me the opportunity to write this book. Finally, without a doubt, I also thank Ann Beardsley for her editorial savvy. Her approach to keeping me on track and not losing "my character" in the editorial process is indeed commendable.

I cannot omit mentioning the gratitude I have for my mentors and my parents (now deceased) for their encouragement during times when I had some misgivings about pursuing a career in teaching.

I will be forever grateful to my students who, after all, were the impetus for this book.

INTRODUCTION

To start such a project as this book seems monumental to me. So many ideas, thoughts, interactions, and experiences must be organized and written with some sort of coherency. Isaac Azimov, the science fiction writer, once told me to begin by putting the words on paper—and that is what I intend to do.

Much has happened in education over the past forty years. Different attitudes and theories of educators (in and out of teaching) have been espoused, the American home scene has changed drastically, and communities' ideas of what a school system should emphasize have been altered incessantly. Obviously, all these variables have had a great influence on those people doing the administering, those people doing the teaching, and youngsters on the "receiving end."

My forty years teaching full-time began in 1957 and ended in 1997, although I continue to teach a summer course and do occasional tutoring. The following is a sketch of the times when I began to teach—just an idea of what was happening in the world at that time, and facts that I believe have had an impact or some influence on education.

In 1957, President Eisenhower was having discussions with Premier Khrushchev about the unveiling of the Russian intercontinental missile; a few weeks later, Sputnik ("traveling companion") was launched. The

Supreme Court's positive decision on school integration and the illegality of bus segregation were declared. This was the era of Dr. Martin Luther King Jr. and the Civil Rights movement.

This was also the time of 3-D movies, hula hoops, droodles, pop-it beads, ducktail haircuts (banned in some schools) for the boys, and poodle cuts for the girls. Certainly, the "music" of any era contains loads of dialogue (messages); such attitudes became more convincing as they were demonstrated by the popular music known as rock and roll! The notorious Elvis Presley sang (?) his "All Shook Up" hit. However, the number one record for 1957 was Debbie Reynolds' "Tammy," and amazing as it is, the popular (to this day) Johnny Mathis was singing his hits: "It's Not for Me to Say" and "Chances Are."

While on the subject, babysitters were 25 cents to $1.25 per hour. I was even able to afford a ballgame now and then and witness the prowess of the "giant" Willie Mays! Finally, a bit of trivia for the auto buffs: in 1962 I purchased a '57 Chevrolet for my wife. Now, I realize my mistake in selling that gem (the auto—not the wife)!

With the above, one acquires the flavor of the '50s, the signature being the "Ding Dong Schools" where Miss Frances clanged the school bell.

There did exist a more stable home than today, where two parents monitored their children and took active consistent roles in the school and community. There was what I refer to as a committed, constructive continuity in the environment. I do believe we are now shifting gears and reexamining what worked so well in "those years."

I plan to touch upon some of the more significant aspects of the above and then to unravel segments of my career—a career full of the proverbial trials and tribulations, the disappointments, the frustrations, the fears, the anxieties, the joys, the ecstasies, and the fun in the classroom. Hopefully, the serious, not so serious, sensitive, touching, endearing, caring, and hilarious aspects of life in and out of the classroom will become evident and informative. I'm sure my personality will be evident and that in itself may (or may not) amuse!

It seems to me to be appropriate that I commence this undertaking at the inception of the Jewish New Year, a time of a new beginning, a sort of awakening in me to share some aspects of my teaching life with others. I am writing for those who contemplate such a life as well as those who enjoy recalling their own experiences in and out of the classroom.

My intent is not necessarily to inform or to instruct but to share with and possibly encourage anyone entertaining the thought of teaching. I hope my insights, observations, and on-the-scene actions will shed some light on what it feels like to be a teacher. Also, I hope that this book will allow a person totally unfamiliar with this profession to develop an understanding and maybe an appreciation for teachers and all they do. All too often, the former students (i.e., the *Homo sapiens* who at one time in their life attended school) now are the authorities, the experts, the "know-it-all people" who manage to command an audience to postulate the antidotes to cure education. After all, if one has managed to attend classes and graduate from a particular institution, one now has a sense of authority to judge all instructors with a fervency. There were no teachers in my family when I began my career, yet many members of my family knew loads about teaching! Their "expertise" could have saved me much tuition, time, and energy! After all, why not "communicate" with these people, receive the pertinent information and move on? Enough of that; I truly do not wish to come across as sarcastic, simply humorous. I must admit, though, that all too often I would succumb to defending myself (or others) and be involved in meaningless "discussions." I'm still wary of self-appointed experts. Although not profound, I hope these readings will spell out the trials and tribulations of the teacher in an honest, sincere manner. In no way are my encounters, episodes, and tales intended to deter one from entering the teaching arena. My intent is simply to relate the "life of the teacher" as it exists in this most wonderfully complex environment. Some parts may astound, some parts may be provocative, some pages may ring some bells, and some pages may turn lights on and open doors. Other pages may slam doors shut—yet all pages are intended to be enlightening for *the teacher who wants to teach* as well as for the nonteacher who knows all about teaching! Many of the names have been changed to maintain confidentiality, but the experiences are truly mine.

My wife is a former teacher and currently a substitute teacher. My son is a seventh-year teacher, his fifth year in a public school system. Put this in perspective and although we Rosenthals do not run our own school, we have some basis of comparison among various systems. I might add that my teaching career was with a single system, from September through June for forty years. I was also privileged to teach summer school in five or six different communities and most recently substituted in a few local elementary schools. Yes, I did see differences and common denominators, and I will combine many of these situations in later scenarios.

Our conversations at the dinner table were saturated with impressions, feelings, and observations; ultimately, opinions and ideas flowed profusely. To be sure, our open honest dialogues meandered like the Charles River and did seem purposeful. My son is grasping the all-too-illusive notion that teaching is not just imparting information. He realizes that patience, sensitivity, compassion, empathy, and humor are part of the arsenal of a teacher. I believe that one must possess these traits to be human first, then add subject matter with a dash of integrity, a spoonful of love, cover this with some spontaneity and gut feelings and voilà, we have some of the ingredients of a teacher with frosting. Not only might this teacher look good, this teacher will feel good (about himself or herself), relate well, and accomplish good . . . but more on this later. I always appreciated Davy Crockett's homespun motto, "Be always sure you are right, then go ahead." These characteristics, some of which are inherited, some learned, and some observed, are all necessary ingredients to being an effective teacher, able to affect young adults! Subject matter and other literacy "tests" are but a single measure and prediction of one's success in the classroom. I believe that, at best, these sorts of high-stakes tests are the minimal barometer, the least important, and by far the most inaccurate measures of a teacher. Indeed, one must have a certain competency in the subject matter one is to teach, yet without the ability to communicate in a variety of methods to a variety of students, the effectiveness and affectiveness is minimal.

You see, when I observed other teachers, I was always concerned with the teacher as a person more so than the lesson: the former revealed more than the latter. Lessons could always be altered, yet the "character" teaching that lesson was paramount to the success of that lesson; I shall expand this a bit later. That character with his or her traits becomes evident as the lessons unfold. Then and only then can one determine if true learning and authentic rapport have been achieved. In no way do I wish to simplify the complicated dynamics that play out in a classroom between teacher and students; I simply want to emphasize the importance of "the person behind the teacher." Teaching credentials are multifaceted; what is not in print is more important (to me) than what is in print.

I also wish to point out that much teaching and learning takes place outside the classroom. I envision the classroom as a "pit stop," a stop where some of the preparations and midcourse corrections take place for the real-life races. How a student is prepared and nurtured in this temporary "holding tank" will determine how well this student will fare in the race. This is more like a relay race where students and teachers are winners by virtue of their working together, their presence, their work ethic, and their perseverance.

I will try to elaborate on the preparation and nurturing, both of which are necessary for teaching and learning to take place. This is a part of the formula for success for both student and teacher. Put teachers who prepare and nurture in safe comfortable environs and we have the makings of an excellent school.

In light of the current (1999–2000) education reforms as far as teacher testing is concerned, yes, I agree that testing is "a" tool, but certainly not the ultimate tool. As you read this book, I hope the anecdotes will corroborate some of my feelings in more detail. I also hope that this book will help beginning teachers to see things in a different light when they step off the merry-go-round. I hope they will look at themselves as a person who cares, who has the capacity to treat people with empathy, and realize they are embarking on a journey that is filled with adventure. The paths of this adventure are going to have detours, U-turns, S-curves, and even stop signs, yet armed with basic human decent feelings (some people call these intangibles), this path will definitely lead to a life full of contentment and love. What a way to go through life! It's been my life and it can be yours also. Ralph Waldo Emerson wrote, "Character is higher than intellect," and if that doesn't say it all, what does?

It was certainly appropriate for President Bush to sign the "new education" bill into law at a public school; indeed, it was clever. President Bush stated on January 8, 2002, that this bill would see to it that "no child will be left behind," hence the No Child Left Behind Act. Yes, accountability is a prime concern as schools are "liberated to meet certain [definite] standards. . . . This bill permits a state to define its own proficiency standards, provided the same standard applies to all students in a grade." Obviously, Congress assumed that accountability was best left to the individual states, and I agree.

At this time in our history, all states should be striving for basic uni-
formity. Indeed, many variables exist, yet communities *must* work for
and achieve a common denominator. This mind-set, this foundation, will
liberate schools to meet standards, according to Dr. Paige, the Secretary
of Education.

The nation will need 2.5 million teachers by 2012 and reforms for
public education are on the way. Along with this combination will come
financing. Congress will appropriate about $22 billion for kindergarten
through twelfth grade for the fiscal year October 2002 to October 2003.
The biggest boosts will come in budgets for teacher training, bilingual
education, reading, and grants to schools with large numbers of poor
children. It is apparent we are now matching the dialogue with the dollar. Teachers are actually hearing "thank you," and their priorities are
being recognized. Funding will increase and we will see a signal of a return to domestic priorities.

President Bush also stated, "These historic reforms will improve our
public schools by creating an environment where every child can learn
through real accountability, unprecedented flexibility for states, and give
school districts greater local control, more options for parents, and more
funding for what works."

I reaffirm what I allude to throughout this book—what a great time it
is to be a part of these reforms *and make a difference in the lives of students*. So, teachers out there, and parents too, take heed—help is on the
way. You will be able to teach and receive your due support. For you
prospective teachers, this should entice you to enter and remain in the
arena and avail yourself of this great opportunity. Look what awaits you:
a government that recognizes your value and talents, and a state that will
follow suit and strive to foster your dreams. I repeat *that now is the time
to teach, if you wish to.*

Now that the teacher and student are in place, the classroom and class
size must follow suit. My classroom was always an extension of my teaching and my personality. Of course, all sorts of significant and not so significant signs, posters, drawings, notes, consumable supplies, and permanent equipment were scattered about in some sort of "decor." Some
items were commercially purchased but most were created by the many
students who individually and collectively decided what work was appropriate to be displayed. I did manage to voice my opinion . . . now and

then. All of these "decorations" made for a comfortable, healthy learning environment. I'm sure many students considered this room their "home away from home," especially when the neatness awards continued to elude us. Contributing to the decor allows students to feel they have a vested interest in the surroundings.

I can unequivocally state that the classroom environment is conducive to learning. This environment, coupled with manageable "numbers," can only enhance the learning process. "Manageable numbers" (to me) means a class size in middle school of a maximum of twenty students per teacher. My equation is: x (the number of pupils) + y (classroom dimension) + z (teacher) = epitome of excellence. Educators must address this three-pronged approach (equation) while not belaboring the "testing."

We must always keep in mind that those candidates or teachers who perform favorably on standardized tests do not guarantee themselves a career in teaching! I suppose I am accustomed to considering more than one aspect of an issue—that way, I have a more informed and, hopefully, a more intelligent opinion.

Through this book, I hope I can alter some attitudes, influence and encourage some minds, and pass some of my enthusiasm on to those who contemplate teaching as well as those in our ranks thinking about leaving.

The majority of my experiences have been limited to the twelve- to fifteen-year-olds, and I have also worked with elementary school children on occasion. Many summers, I taught high school students and I enjoyed a brief (two-year) experience working with college students.

Approximately seventeen years ago, my "tag" of teaching junior high (grades seven through nine) ended and the updated version in this process of modern academic education became the tag of teaching middle school (grades six through eight). These junior high/middle schoolers turned me on. (I shall not refer to my own children at this time—be patient!) These wild, confused, insecure, immature, and awkward adolescents craved for and deserved much attention. I have often thought that these adolescents were more honest and sincere than many adults. They are more open and amenable to discovery and come with no preconceived biases—only short-lived misconceptions.

I was always amused by the late Erma Bombeck's words on adolescents when she said, "Don't ever say you understand them. It breaks down the

hostile relationship between you that it takes to understand one another."
My feelings were enhanced when I read Dr. Bernie Siegel's book *Pre-scriptions for Living* where he stated that, "Prophets and storytellers all advise us to be more childlike. Children teach us about honesty and feelings. They show us how to be loving in the face of adversity."

As soon as I met my students in the early morning, my own thoughts were preempted as I was compelled to listen to their "more pressing" thoughts. My problems seemed to disappear as I tried to understand the urgencies that were imminent (at least) to them. Their problems didn't compound mine; on the contrary, I now had the opportunity to help them. What a great feeling to try to make a difference in the life of a youngster who is asking for help! And this "help" may or may not have any connection to teaching—but it does to learning!

Who is this special person who comes into their life, this person who will devote his or her life to cultivating and nurturing these adolescents? Who is this person who will assist them in their struggle for independence, their difficulties in discovering their identity, and their growing emotionally, physically, socially, and intellectually; and even impart some subject matter? Easy! This special person is their *teacher*. Talk about responsibility all you want; to me, this is the epitome of it. Put in these terms, the teacher is indeed in a powerful, awesome position. Do student teachers (many barely out of adolescence themselves) fully comprehend their task, their charge, their responsibility? I do not think so! Maybe if they did, they would rethink priorities. Yet, I say, bless them for trying, bless them for not listening to those pessimists, bless them for putting their feelings and beliefs before their material needs. If these interns are committed to a work ethic and a need to connect family and community, their material world will be realized in due time; mine was.

I'm reminded of Freud who stated that love and work are the two things a mature person has to be able to do well. I say teaching helps one develop maturity and certainly all aspects of love are prerequisite to good teaching. I mention all aspects of love because, as Tolstoy mentions, there is love of country, love of family, love of flag, even love of teacher; in other words, different kinds of love.

Rabbi Kushner believes that "if we are lucky, we will find ourselves at a place in life when we can derive pleasure from our work." Yes indeed; I believe I would only change the word "lucky" to "fortunate": I have arrived!

I would hope education students choose to become teachers and not let other influences shape their goals. Dr. Seigel said, "Making the choices by yourself and following through is more difficult, yet much more gratifying and satisfying." I do believe one needs encouragement, yet loving something (after loving oneself) is a great beginning.

Increasingly, I hear from teachers who tell me they are unhappy with their work. Many can hardly wait to leave their current position. In the meantime, much dissatisfaction, ambivalence, and animosity abounds, creating a most unhealthy environment. I like to believe (and I hope it's not naiveté) that these teachers are in the minority.

I also have heard the battle cry of teachers who claim to have the ideal occupation because "We are off during the summer months and check out our vacations." I say these teachers (?) do not have the ideal occupation. If that is their criteria of an ideal occupation, we are all heading for trouble. What about the nonteacher who exclaims, "You teachers have all these vacations!"

To the credit of our country, in this new millennium, we will witness better training in addition to more stringent monitoring of teachers and curriculum. In combination with additional funds and smaller class sizes, these will be the prescriptions to cure the ills that plague many a school system.

As far as teacher monitoring is concerned, I've always realized that constructive criticism in this process is of great value. Teachers become less apprehensive of the process and are able to learn from their mistakes. After all, isn't this one of the tenets of any worthwhile endeavor? I always appreciated sincere, honest evaluations in my own career because the discussions that followed proved fruitful.

Dr. Richard Carlson states in his book *Don't Sweat the Small Stuff*,

> Most of us struggle against the idea that our ideas don't always match those of other people. We get angry, hurt and frustrated when people reject our ideas . . . or give us some other form of disapproval. . . . The sooner we accept the inevitable dilemma of not being able to win the approval of everyone we meet (and everything we do), the easier our lives will become.

Thank goodness, as I grew professionally, my bank account grew and my children grew healthy, while my wife and I witnessed such events. What a joyous ride! In other words, I continued to work hard and reap rewards, tangible as well as intangible. For me, both were necessary—or to be more exact, vital.

I

THE "PLANT"

❶

SPACE: IN AND OUT OF SCHOOL

Just like a school, this chapter will follow a general floor plan with the usual amenities—lighting, lockers, corridors, drinking fountains, rest rooms, cafeteria, a myriad of classrooms, library, gymnasium, exercise and/or weight training room and showers, and various offices such as guidance, special needs, and of course, the main office with all sorts of secretarial staff for the principal, assistant principals, nurses, other visiting dignitaries, and a teachers' room (certainly not one of the best furnished). This list comprises obvious visible areas of the plant, but for the moment we won't delve into the boiler room and kitchen areas. There must also be space provided for the specialists who divide their time among different schools within the system. One cannot forget the superb assistance the custodial staff provides, a staff that is oft times delegated to work out of a closet, for the most part. I often expected to open a closet door and have a custodian fall out, sort of like a "Fibber McGee" arrangement! (For those of you readers too young to remember, "Fibber McGee and Molly" was a humorous vaudeville radio show that ran from 1935 to 1959.)

Space is an important commodity in most schools. The usual buzzword is overcrowding, where too many bodies are seemingly occupying the same area at the same precise time of day. Teachers live with the fact

that they are outnumbered twenty or twenty-five to one in close quarters. Not such a horrific ratio when one considers that not too long ago
twenty-five or thirty to one was the norm, and I'm sure this ratio still exists in many a community. Full-time aides (many of whom are certified
teachers) are sometimes hired when student/teacher ratios reach a certain level.

A note on space as it pertains to discipline: Heaven forbid that a student who on any given day might be quarantined (for whatever reason)
or given an in-house suspension and must be assigned to a conference
room or even the principal's office. We might as well assign this unfortu-
nate youngster to the cafeteria for an additional meal, and keep this student happy and content while on detention. Many a student, sent to the
main office for discipline, usually finds himself greeting visitors and automatically enrolled as an office aide; perhaps we have discovered an in-
novative method of "dealing with discipline!" (More on discipline later.)

Many a time, walls and windows are rearranged to accommodate dis-
orderly students. It is the responsibility of the teacher to manage discipline, and sending the student to the office may not be the best route to
take. We all realize that without discipline, nothing is ever accomplished; however, at this time I shall elude only to the "whereabouts" of
the disciplined. The teacher (disciplinarian) must assume the total responsibility of housing this youngster. Often, the teacher has no option
but to keep the student in her classroom, and may well begin to appreciate the fact that "regular" classes are not necessarily the mainstay of
the classroom.

Then there is "sharing" of space, a fact that puts a great strain on
teachers and students. Can one imagine a prospective teacher asking if
the classroom is to be shared and the response is positive (for the room
sharing)? Is the teacher to accept or reject the position on this basis?

Many communities have a definite upward trend in student population. At times, school systems find that, after constructing new schools,
they are filling the schools faster than anticipated, meaning they might
be at capacity by the time they open. More room and additional staff are
needed, but on the positive side, at least *some* of the additional students
were planned for.

Some communities are converting certain nonclassroom areas to
classrooms; some have rented and built modular classrooms and leased

buildings. All have undertaken to reduce class size and thereby address a very important issue in education: the teacher/student ratio. As communities change, we see old antiquated classrooms give way to newer, more modern, state-of-the-art buildings that accommodate the increased enrollment and influx of twenty-first-century technology and teaching methods.

After all, we have come a long way from the likes of Granby, Vermont, a town that is proud of their one-room elementary school that has one teacher and nine students. Still, not a bad student-teacher ratio for a city population of ninety!

Do "outsiders" ever consider what educators mean when they say space is limited, overcrowding exists, and many schools are over their capacity? Schools are probably the only institutions that are expected to function properly and maintain standards with such disadvantages. In several schools, the commodities taken for granted are luxuries to others: language laboratories, up-to-date computer facilities, modern science equipment, and music rooms and auditoriums (in some schools, often one and the same with the gymnasium) with acoustical enhancements. We'll talk more about the classroom itself in chapter 2.

Oh yes, if space (here, that is) permits, I may touch upon the environs including the parking or nonparking facilities: parking meters. That might be the answer, possibly another method of raising funds. Who knows, the next school newspaper headline could read MRBS (Meters Replace Bake Sale)! However, trivial as it first appears, parking can be an issue around many a school. The newer schools (that is, those built within the last few years) have ample, easily accessible areas. Unfortunately, the majority of schools either have a sparse area for parking or an area that is not in close proximity to the school. The parking situation even governs the teachers' schedules as well. The early birds, as usual, occupy the choice spaces, nearly abutting the building. The late arrivals might contend with a five- to seven-minute trek. For some, this exercise is welcome, yet others are not so pleased, especially during inclement weather. I've visited schools where the spaces are numbered and the teachers with longevity are afforded a numbered space nearly atop the school. Translated into practicality, this means if the teacher has been on the staff for forty years, that teacher's parking space is within thirty seconds from auto to classroom! I have always wondered where the beginning teacher parked at those schools.

This mere act of parking a car not only involves time, it often involves weight-lifting exercises. Some of us do have homework (just like the students) and this necessitates carrying texts/manuscripts, equipment, and possibly lunch (the bagged variety). This is certainly not a major concern, merely something every teacher has to consider; however, it's one additional item for teachers to plan, similar to staying in shape!

2

THE CLASSROOM

The classroom is the room with all the action. There are situations where this classroom is moved elsewhere, yet for now I will consider the variety with walls, ceiling, desks, tables, chairs, wall boards, bulletin boards, lighting, and so forth, and most often windows, but not always. Many times, the teacher's desk, chair, and file cabinet are part of—you could not have guessed—the classroom. Not all professionals have an office or anyplace that even resembles an office. Teachers set up all sorts of barricades on and around their desk—possibly to hide, possibly to resemble a fortress, or possibly to achieve some sort of privacy. Can one imagine maintaining an office in the midst of a classroom? Teachers can. There is one advantage to this: the private telephone cannot be placed in the immediate vicinity of this "office." Why, it could ring or buzz or beep (as in professional offices) in the midst of a class or meeting! I'm sure someone out there could figure out the teacher's schedule and call when no class is in session but even then, the classroom may be occupied by more than one teacher on any given day. Perhaps we should turn this problem over to the computer programmers.

The "telephone" that often has a presence in the classroom is the interschool communication system. This system is as important as the clock.

Certainly, bulletin boards, white boards, and chalkboards are all considered basic necessities and where they are situated is as important as having the appropriate furniture for the students. Obviously, certain disciplines (such as music, science, languages, physical education, and arts and crafts) require special furniture (and space) unique to the course. Ventilation and lighting are also important considerations, both of which must be factored into this confinement in order to have a healthy (physical and mental) learning environment. Remember, this is where the action takes place and there must not be any distractions, or at least any excuses for distractions! It is the responsibility of the teacher to make this environment conducive to teaching and learning.

This "prime property" becomes what I refer to as "public domain." Spot a room with no class occupying same; don't question, simply move in! (A mentality practiced by many.) I was on one of my local field trips around the grounds of the school collecting insects with my classes, and I had visions of my temporarily vacant classroom being taken over by another teacher in search of space! Sounds ridiculous, yet I did have a few close calls. Would it have been appropriate to post a sign on the door stating "Out, be back at . . ."!?

I also have vivid memories of "room sharing." This sounds so fraternal, but I must dispel this notion of brotherly love. I remember my ongoing feuds with a math teacher, two English teachers, and a special reading teacher. I know there were others but I do not want to come across as the award winner for "feudalism" (in this context)! Built into my schedule were specific periods on certain days when these teachers would move in, and that they did. Because I taught science at the time, I would make sure no leftover experiment was visible or in human range (almost an impossibility) out of my concern to avoid catastrophic consequences. The reader must not forget this was "my" room—or so I thought. It was only my room for certain parts of the day and week, as matters turned out.

Now, I can fully appreciate a juggling act: where to put what when, or when to put what where, or what to put where when! Is this an environment conducive to learning, with no distractions? Will teachers, many new to the arena, be exposed to such circumstances? Seems to me these kinds of juggling acts belong in the circus, certainly not in the school setting. *However*, remember the words that relay messages of devotion, love, and commitment to one's work . . . in spite of adversity!

I finally left the bargaining table with a small victory. At the very least, the boards (chalk and white) were cleared prior to my grand entrance and I did not allow the students to roll my (teacher's) chair down the corridor. Teachers do aim to cooperate, and the above was accomplished. Before long, we were all as compatible as a family moving into a new home together, each of us staking out our individual turf.

The teachers who "shared" my classroom with me were fortunate to have also experienced other pleasures, namely my little blue parakeet who was at home in this aviary. You will recognize that the teachers' classroom should be an extension of the teacher—the teacher's personality, the teacher's character, the teacher's identity, and the teacher's individuality. The sum of such qualities will add up to one dedicated, devoted, and interesting person. Now back to our pet parakeet. I trained this little one to remain in the classroom, even when the door was open. She would leave her cage, land on different tables or desks, once in a while peck on some paper, and once in a while "do her business" on a table! This bird was the mascot of the classes and not a day would pass without students looking forward to caressing her. This was one bird that could not be kept in her cage during the day, and she did welcome the petting—petting by students who, for the first time in their lives, touched such a creature. This pet had a soothing, comforting effect on several students, especially during exams! At first glance, one would think our mascot was distracting students from their work; however, I soon observed the opposite was true. Too bad I didn't do some sort of relevant research project and quantify results. Now this is an idea for a future thesis: it's up for grabs.

I was fortunate to be a member of a teaching team assigned to students whose country of origin spanned the world. Approximately 25 percent of our students (on a team of about one hundred students) were born and experienced elementary education in countries other than the United States. What a great opportunity for us all to share in this diversity that spanned all continents. To expand my enthusiasm and enhance this welcoming of students, I solicited the help of team members (students) to construct flags of the country of origin of each of these students and, in some cases, the flag of a grandparent's country of birth.

With this accomplished, these flags spanned nearly fifty feet across the classroom—a teaching and learning experience, to be sure. The newly gained knowledge, respect for tolerance, and respect for diversity are a definition of education. To repeat myself slightly, I wanted to emphasize to the students that as we live and learn in this great country of ours, it's up to each one of us to work and study to the best of our ability, and the teacher is here to assist you to do just that!

For those teachers who occupy a classroom of "their own," be grateful, be thankful, be generous and kind, and above all, do not take this luxury for granted!

It seems in order to pay homage to those fantastic physical education teachers and "their" classroom. Obviously, their classroom is most often the gymnasium and, by extension, the "field." This gymnasium is also shared with other coaches and teachers. Often, teachers sponsor activities that require the facilities (and space) of this environment. I am reminded of several events—science and international fairs, spelling bees, exhibitions, award programs, and graduation ceremonies—that are often conducted there. Naturally, the setting was conducive for these activities to take place, and it was a plus for us to avail ourselves of its use.

Because I am mentioning activities other than the usual athletic programs, it becomes obvious that the gym appeals to the entire school community and is probably the busiest "classroom."

Often, teams that depend on the goddess of weather (Meteore?) must alter their plans and naturally opt to practice in the gym. I recall introducing my tennis team to the gym for much needed practice and discovering the need to share the area with the track team. Can you imagine hitting tennis balls while runners and jumpers are about? I mentioned to the track coach that my tennis team should receive some credit for improving the high-jumping prowess of his athletes! This is another classic example of cooperation among the players . . . and teachers. I will certainly not elaborate on the sessions we conducted when the baseball battery entered the picture! I believe they did catch a few tennis balls . . . in the glove!

All these incidents are elaborated here to illustrate the complexities of planning and sharing within the limitations of space. Some schools live with the fact of gym *and* auditorium being one and the same.

Locker rooms are a given when we refer to physical education, an additional area that must be monitored. The playing (athletic) field, another given, is the "extension" of this classroom, and is also used by many students throughout the day for classes and the usual after-school sports teams. It becomes quite easy to understand and appreciate why the physical education teacher and his classroom deserve a place in the sun!

I mentioned interschool communication earlier and hinted at some elaboration. This technology—especially the type that emanated from a loudspeaker system—was a thorn in my side, my back, my feet, my arm, and my head. The telephone-type of intercom assures a subtly and privacy that can at least be tolerated, but was rarely the chosen device!

I will never understand why office staff and others believe that classrooms can be interrupted at any time of the day, except for the one time that seems to be sacred: when the standardized (sanitized) tests are administered. At this time, the world becomes instantly silent, as though a master audio switch was thrown and even the faintest whisper could not be detected.

If I were to list a few of my most annoying situations, the incessant intercom interruptions would probably rank near (if not at) the top of the list. I can understand emergencies; however, when I'm interrupted to relay to Joshua that his mother will be unavailable to escort him to the orthodontist. . . . What about the time when I was reminded to remind Elisabeth to remind her brother, who was on a field trip, to remember not to forget his key! This may all sound amusing, but this does happen. I find this deplorable and demeaning to the teacher. I do take it personally because I feel there is a lack of respect . . . for the teaching!

On several occasions, I would make my trek to the office, state my case, be given sympathy (not called for), and be assured that some effort would be made to curtail these interruptions . . . all to no avail! This was, however, the subject for a faculty meeting . . . title being "Is There Anything Sacred?" It seemed as though I had loads of company, but this did not make the misery any easier. As the year progressed, I believe I did make some inroads in spite of the inevitable announcements. There was no war, yet I had succeeded in winning a small battle, and that helped. Teachers! Be prepared to stand up for what you think is right and, as usual, justice will prevail.

❸

THE LIBRARY

The library is a very important sanctuary for some and one of the core locations for acquiring information for others. What a great place to do research, do "homework," and even learn how to use the facilities. With the librarians and the fantastic resources, including the technology, this place is truly the information highway. Of course, where else could one meet friends, copy homework, read a magazine or newspaper, all in close proximity? Some students even find refuge in the "stacks," a sort of home away from home. It is the responsibility of the classroom teachers to monitor what their students are doing in this environment.

I remember Ashley who seemed to spend more time in the library than the librarians. If I equated her time in these environs with her academic progress, her grades would far surpass those of her classmates; however, this was definitely not the case—but this was a case . . . for a sleuth! (I have always maintained that in addition to other teaching credentials, the teacher should acquire some training in the realm of a detective.)

Well, Ashley used her ingenuity (?) to set up her arrival time to coincide with her boyfriend's arrival. Nothing new, yet they both added a few alterations to their plans that confused teachers for a time. I did sort out their "comings and goings" and put an end to this devious behavior. I took advantage of the situation to review some ideas with them on honesty, reliability, responsibility, and integrity, and also explained how important it was to know of their whereabouts in case of an emergency in the event of a call from home or possibly a fire drill. These matters never occurred to her and my lack of trust in her was heightened. I hope she realized my disappointment

Students should be allowed to take full advantage of such facilities while exchanging ideas. This facility provides a forum for collaboration with people in and outside of the school and is a wonderful place to speak, listen, and learn. It is the teacher's responsibility to enhance such activities while some semblance of order is maintained.

On several occasions, my classes were conducted in this environment. How does one approach a research project? Where to begin? Where to search? What (re)sources are available? Which sources to include and to what extent? Many questions are spawned in these environs and students learn the process involved in investigating and reporting.

Planning is important—planning ahead for the students *and* the teachers. It is necessary to warn (just kidding?) the librarians and reserve the time, with reasonable notice of the desire to use the facilities. This also assists the library staff to ready any materials the teacher wishes to be available. Organization is a key word in any teacher's life. It is an unwritten rule that all teachers, beginning and veterans, must adhere to. Failing to do so is certainly considered out of the bounds of professionalism. I'm absolutely sure that this rule needs no elaboration for it will become quite evident early on in one's career.

I remember an occasion when Holocaust survivors spoke with classes in this most appropriate environment because a wealth of information could be found here. This is the place surrounded with literature and opinions, convictions and facts, about men and women whose lives have shaped our world. What an ideal location to explore, to investigate, and to read, *and to listen to life*.

I also witnessed a forum-like setting involving several classes and an AIDS awareness program. One of my better experiences was listening to "senior" citizens ranging in age from approximately seventy to eighty years young. Several tables were occupied, each with one senior and a group of students discussing many issues of the "times back then." Andy Rooney once said that the best classroom in the world is at the feet of an elderly person. To think I could (nearly) be the guest speaker at one of those tables now is indeed mind boggling to me!

The library is noted for its "open appeal," sort of everyone's classroom. Teachers and various specialists can always be seen working with small groups of students. Teachers can also be seen reading the newspapers and magazines, similar to other humans in the public library! And these same teachers might even be seen conversing (quietly, of course) with their colleagues. Most staff meetings are scheduled in this environment. Many social events occur here and, at times, a school committee meeting will be conducted here.

Obviously, all students should be trained in the proper use of the library, from using the card files to the latest research techniques and use of the computers; sort of a minicourse in library science.

I was always aware of the library's proposed purchases and I encouraged my colleagues to do likewise. Librarians are amenable to the idea of teachers suggesting appropriate books (for purchase) in their subject. If the library's budget permits, such books are added to the stacks. What a neat opportunity to get what you want while someone else pays the bill! But think twice before exercising this technique elsewhere!

Parents often arrive for different events scheduled to take place in the library. Their children may be reciting an original poem or reiterating a scene from *Macbeth* or possibly debating with classmates "on this process of academic education." Whatever the activity, just the ambiance of the library makes the school community proud. I believe when a person visits the school's library, that person acquires a feeling of what the school is about, similar to visiting a public library in any community. I would invite readers to try this. That is, visit a city or town with which one might not be too familiar and seek out the library. Try to form an opinion "about the community." Were you correct or close to being correct?

For me, the library was the heart of the plant, the core of the reactor, the battery of the auto, and the wherewithal to forge ahead with one's education.

4

COMMON SPACES

Now this chapter is a conglomeration of several duties, and that's no pun! To patrol a corridor, a teacher must be alert and astute, have a few educational degrees, and yet not appear to be a police officer. And don't forget the sense of humor!

After forty years of teaching, the most asked question is still, "Can I go to the bathroom?" It took several years for students to learn to ask, "*May* I go to the bathroom?"! At times, I thought there was an epidemic of bladder infections (but at this age?) or possibly malfunctioning of the digestive tract (but at this age?), until I finally realized the bathroom was just another refuge for some students. After all, the addiction to nicotine was much more intense than that of gum chewing or the necessity for urinating. It is the responsibility of the teacher to monitor this site periodically for obvious reasons. This home away from home (to several students) is not the most pleasant area to police (pardon the expression), yet is a necessary task.

Drinking fountains can be a blessing for students as well as for teachers but they can and do present problems, especially when students are moving about the corridor. I was always amazed that more students were not hurt with chipped teeth or cut lips as the heavy traffic made for close quarters. Leaning forward to drink and having several people brushing by could be "the accident waiting to happen." The students might be filing into the teacher's own classroom, yet this teacher must be aware of the corridor scene . . . simultaneously (at times), with one foot inside and the other foot outside the door.

Lockers are certainly a necessity, especially when students wish to store seasonal clothing (that may or may not belong to them) and, of course, as a place to store last week's lunch! I did manage to see some textbooks piled and literally stuffed in compartments that gave meaning to that Fibber McGee scene. The bottom line was that the majority of these adolescents don't think about sanitation or house cleaning until the days of reckoning (i.e., clean-out time prior to vacations or the final school days), provided their olfactory nerves haven't tipped them off sooner.

Adam was the kind of kid who would hoard everything from pens, pencils, and erasers to clothes he never wore and books he never read, to lunches and other food he either forgot he had or didn't wish to eat. It was the rations, the foodstuffs, the cuisine, and the edibles that were stored along with the aforementioned nonperishables that came to my attention.

There were hundreds of lockers in that school, and I had the (mis)fortune to teach in a classroom that bordered this stockpile of pure trash, a haven that certainly would have been condemned whenever discovered. Perishables that are left unattended or improperly cared for will eventually arouse one's suspicions, to say the least! I had Adam open his questionable sanctuary (?) and it was now his turn to practice using such utensils and ingredients as brushes, sponges, wipes, cloths, deodorizers, soap, and a battery of scouring pads. To see this youngster wearing a sanitary mask, gloves, and an apron was indeed a picture for the yearbook. Adam didn't quite make the yearbook edition; however, I did threaten him with the idea that *Good Housekeeping* magazine might give him some billing! Another lesson learned, and think how pleased his parents were when informed of Adam's latest state of accountability.

I must admit though that the library was grateful for the discovery of several lost books, losses that have caused many a teacher and student much grief. I do hope today's teachers are prepared to supervise these locker clean-outs with some sort of savvy-nose plugs, rubber gloves, and . . . a giant barrel! More later on trying to decipher the combination locks (combinations kept with the teacher) and, of course, the caretaking of the keys for those youngsters who feel their locker is synonymous with Fort Knox.

I hope the teacher comes prepared to open a file on lockers for the inevitable discussion will ensue. "I can't remember my number" or "I can't find my key." This could involve many students who chose to share and share alike (lockers). Combination locks are a tricky sort of device, especially if one must deal with the numerous varieties. The teacher *will* become an amateur locksmith as the school year progresses. Some initially turn clockwise, others turn counterclockwise. Remember to pass one number, stop at another number, and keep in mind which direction to proceed and where to stop.

Students invariably request your help just as you are going to a meeting or during your fifteen- to twenty-minute lunch break. You follow the student's directions, play with all the numbers, and the lock still doesn't open! You are definitely sympathetic because this student's lunch is fastened behind the metal door and in no way are you going to have a repeat performance à la Adam. You, the teacher, try and try again until those little numbers line up like the cross hairs on a scope, and open sesame it is. Whew!

Of course, now the teacher is left with a dilemma: which is the more pressing, the excursion to the rest room or the trip to the cafeteria (to eat, not on duty)? Keep in mind the time has elapsed and the clock is down to twelve to fifteen minutes for both "activities." People may find this scenario amusing, but every teacher *will* experience this and it *will not* be so amusing.

To observe a student interrupt his gait in the corridor and suddenly leap in the air, as though defying gravity, and succeed in hitting the lens of a light fixture is indeed a talent that must be brought to the attention of the track coach. Keeping in mind what I said about sense of humor, self-control, and the number of degrees one has, some sort of communication between student and teacher is in order, immediate or deferred.

I observed Sam early in the year skip down the corridor and in an instant become airborne, only to miss tapping the light lens, his intended target. With much frustration, this same act was repeated daily as he came in close proximity to my classroom. To him, it was a ritual; to me,

amusing . . . for a time. I must admit that I was silently cheering for him
to "reach" his goal. And reach it he did, after nearly six months. His persistence paid off with, of course, the help of his growth hormones. I also
was present to witness this great achievement (hence the inclusion of
this episode) when the lens was finally hit. It cracked along with a section of tile board from the surrounding ceiling area. Sam's instant pirou-
ette forced him to come face to face with me and our eyes met. I asked
him if he was satisfied with the initial part of his triumph, ignoring for
now the consequences of his follow through! Finally we zeroed in on the
"now what does he intend to do about the necessary repairs." I was de-
lighted to listen to Sam offer his idea for restitution. He offered no excuses and said he would speak with a custodian regarding the clean up
and repayment process. Bravo to this student who assumed responsibility for his actions. Subsequently, the custodian asked what I might know
about the incident and "we" concluded that accidents do happen, lessons
are learned, and above all, no one was hurt. You now know the outcome.

I do want to add that in no way did I influence the decision process.
The decision was agreed upon with a mutual respect and understanding.
I know this young man would admit to any transgression, even if there
were no witnesses. I believe Sam adheres to the old adage that honesty
is the best policy.

I have always felt that much is to be learned in the environs of the corridor. The majority of the time must be devoted to listening, and observing, with a segment devoted to trying to say the right thing at the
right time. . . . Remember when I eluded to one's teacher training? Forget looking for the proper responses in the teaching manuals—there are
none! There exists many a situation where gut feelings take over and
these built-in behavior patterns are reliable and viable options to exercise. In other words, *go for it*!

Many of these situations might seem trivial to one unfamiliar with the
life of the teacher, but they do exist and they must be dealt with. To be
sure, they are mundane occurrences in the school setting but the teachers who apply their love, compassion, and honesty to this environment
will forever be successful.

5

THE CAFETERIA

The cafeteria is not the place for the queasy or the meticulous. Imagine a place where all human emotions and feelings are in motion simultaneously, embodied in hundreds of teenagers. Just say a few prayers when the schedules are printed that you, at the very least, have some unassigned time either prior to (preferably) or following cafeteria duty. If one wants to lose weight, this is the alternative to exercise. Watching many adolescents eat (?) is in itself a horrifying view. For a few moments, one witnesses some civility at the tables and suddenly remnants of a sandwich are airborne; at another table, several students carry on as though this gastronomical feast were the last meals of their short lifetimes. The proverbial shovel should be the appropriate utensil for the meal as one watches these young *homo sapiens* devour food.

There are students who have various clean-up responsibilities and this activity has much merit. I'm not sure how many youngsters have such chores to do at home but for many, this is the place where the initial exposure to cleaning up after themselves occurs. Here again is a learning situation that involves a certain amount of decorum along with manners. The teachers who are fortunate to have witnessed "lunchtime" can now be proud of themselves for having survived another phase of school life. After all, cafeteria duty may well be the pinnacle of accomplishment, to be obtained only with the completion of a bachelor's degree and, in many instances, a master's degree.

A definite amount of patience and skill is necessary to manage a shift of approximately 150 to 200 students in a time span of twenty to twenty-five minutes; even the military might take a lesson from our middle school kids. Now just imagine having all of these hungry cherubs seated and ready to line up for their options. Some come fortified with the proverbial brown bags because they have decided that the cafeteria food is just not to be in their realm. Others (the brave?) have taken the easy route: the food line. Of course, following this line comes the dessert line. With about a total of five to seven minutes waiting factored into the duration of the lunch period, this amounts to fifteen to eighteen minutes of actual devouring time. Students who otherwise claim to have trouble communicating suddenly allow time to discuss worldly issues in between (and sometimes during) bites. If one wishes to observe students moving with excessive haste, visit the entry to the cafeteria. However, to witness slow motion in action, simply acquaint yourself with the exit sign.

Cafeteria duty is a necessary activity that demands much attention and supervision, an activity that has a built-in priority when the complex scheduling ensues, an activity that invariably involves much of the staff's time and energy, and the activity that elicits the least amount of appreciation and accolades.

Many a teacher has completed her cafeteria assignment for the day, only to feel exhausted and unloved, but must still get on with the teaching. Maybe that advanced degree was a necessary document to have earned in order to deal with all the strange and complex intricacies taking place in the cafeteria.

6

HOMEROOM

This must be one of the most colorful and busy times in a teacher's day. My files were constantly being updated—by the hour! My favorite file will always consist of the "excuse notes." This file deserves a place in the sun, as the poets write. Most were written by parents and guardians, some were written by older or younger siblings, and a few were signed by authors of unknown origin. It is this last category that turned yours truly into a sleuth, one comparable to the inimitable Sherlock Holmes.

A student would turn in the note, "late" with an illegible signature for a tardy, and this document was supposed to absolve him from the infraction of the rules. An excuse might state "sick" (scribbled on a 2"× 4" card) with no visible signature, following a few days of absences. I was not really looking for an entire diagnosis or daily symptoms, merely some indication that there existed no communicable disease and that the student had seen a doctor.

Then we have the excuse essays. One student was tardy and the mom wrote that her younger child hid the car keys. When these were retrieved, the car wouldn't start. Waiting for AAA consumed another thirty minutes and a stop over at the elementary school to deposit another sibling was in order. At this point, nature took over and mom made another pit stop prior to delivering the last precious cargo to yours truly.

I always gave students the benefit of any doubt I had when I read their absentee or tardy excuses. However, there was one student who spotted this trait in me and took advantage of my generosity.

Amanda was always polite and willing to assist me with any chores during her homeroom period. I took advantage of her offers to organize the books and help me conserve the all-important space. She did this and managed several other details that I dreaded to tackle. Teachers look for such "help" and it is a blessing to find a capable and willing student who runs the risk of being labeled "teacher's pet." Because Amanda was given a certain amount of freedom during homeroom, she (mistakenly) thought such freedom was extended to other areas, most notably, note writing and signing. When excuses for absenteeism and tardiness were handed to me, I would glance at the note, look for a signature, and file the note, a process that became routine. Once I was satisfied with the excuse itself and there was nothing truly personal, I delegated the task of filing the notes to Amanda. After a few weeks elapsed, I noticed that Amanda couldn't wait to resume this particular activity and that the script of the "different" signatures seemed to be aligned and arranged in a similar slant (pattern). The excuses, especially the ones relating to tardiness, seemed to be coming from the same few families with the same few excuses. Everything seemed too perfect, almost as though these notes were stamped out from a production line. I decided to speak with Amanda before calling any parents and guardians, and after my own investigations and a closer look at the notes, I confronted Amanda. Loads of tears (Amanda's), much apologizing, and genuine remorse followed.

My biggest decision was determining appropriate consequences for her actions and the actions of her accomplices. Initially, Amanda and I had a discussion about honesty and trust, and I relayed my deep feeling of how these two principles of human behavior are tantamount to one's character and integrity, principles that *must* be accepted and practiced if one is to become a respected and useful citizen. Amanda and her cohorts met with me and could easily determine how disappointed I was with them. I was also insulted by their actions and made quite evident the severity of such offenses.

These three girls were to write an essay, individually, explaining the meaning of honesty and integrity, using specific examples in their own lives and in the lives of others. I wanted them to include interviews with people who exemplify such qualities. I wanted them to come to some conclusions based on their own observations and interviews. I also demanded that they complete this "assignment" before explaining the history that precipitated the essay to their parents and guardians. Lastly, they were to meet, once again, with me individually, and relate to me what they included in their writings. Their oral dissertation was to include *all* requirements I spelled out for them, including, of course, *their* conclusions.

Amanda was relieved of her responsibilities helping me and I remember her genuine efforts throughout the remainder of the school year trying to and succeeding in restoring my faith in her and her friends.

There does come the time to reiterate the basic rules of the school, and the handbook usually spells out many of the expectations. This is a sort of an updated version of the bible with loads of variations and "individual interpretations."

All students receive a handbook, yet whether this is opened is a totally different story. Therefore, the homeroom teacher has the responsibility to review and reiterate some of the rules that might be overlooked. This activity is certainly not a top priority for many teachers; however, soon the teacher realizes that this chore will become part of a "lesson plan" for homeroom sessions. The teacher's particular degree will not help unless one has had some training in legal jargon.

About this time, the teacher and homeroom students usually develop a mutual closer bond than regular classrooms. The homeroom becomes their home away from home. There exists an informal, comfortable, and chaotic atmosphere where much learning does take place—learning for the teacher as well as the students.

Now for some of the specific rules and regulations.

Freedom of Petition is one of my favorite rules because this allows students to collect signatures on petitions concerning either in-school or out-of-school issues as long as this activity does not interfere with the regular operations of classes. For some students, wearing hats in class and around school is an issue. These same students are not entirely discreet about advocating their opinions, yet they are willing to support the cause whether or not class might be interrupted. A great lesson in democracy at work, if only these students could transfer this skill to their own lives in and out of school. It's the old adage of putting these energies to work on some of their more immediate and important concerns. This Freedom of Expression is great as long as the teacher assists in channeling this freedom in the right direction.

Rules of Behavior and Discipline of Students truly require that legal degree I mentioned earlier. A student's civil rights must be considered as provided in the Fifth and Fourteenth Amendments to the U.S. Constitution, and this is where the term "due process" comes from. Therefore, if a student is facing suspension, she is protected by the Due Process Clause of the Fourteenth Amendment (a ruling of the U.S. Supreme Court in 1975).

There are rules for suspension of ten days or less and ten days or more, there are regulations for appeals, there are rules for expulsion and involuntary transfers. Many schools also have policy statements on drug, alcohol, and tobacco use and abuse. In addition to this, there also exist various disciplinary consequences related to these as well as attendance, hazing, and sexual harassment.

I have mentioned a few of the "handbook inclusions" that must be taken seriously by all parties to help maintain a safe and civil environment for learning. As stated in our handbook, "School should be a setting in which respect for rules and common decency are accepted by all as the necessary structure for both learning and community, and where those in authority try always to strike a balance between individual rights and the general good."

I believe disciplining students is an art and a talent that cannot always be taught. It is such an individual "activity" that it requires the proverbial on-the-job training. The amount and type of education a teacher has had is not directly proportional to the effectiveness of the disciplining. Yes, it does take practice (there will certainly be ample opportunities!) and a certain amount of that "gut" feeling to do the right thing. I remember my class at Harvard Summer School many, many years ago, where several students tried desperately to have the professor advise them how and what discipline should be administered in specific situations! I always wondered if those students ever made it to the classroom and, if they did, to what extent were they successful. I did sympathize with their feelings and anxieties; however, even at that time, I knew there could not be any satisfactory answers.

There are as many methods of discipline as there are numbers of students . . . and then some. This is such a personal evaluation with so many variables to consider, the teacher would find it difficult to come to the table with a set of hard-and-fast rules. Without writing an essay on the subject, I must add that this is where all teachers draw on their experiences, skills, maturity, patience, courage, and wisdom.

Usually, the daily bulletins and announcements are broadcast during homeroom. A time to hear, a time to listen, a time to decipher the various messages and be ready to siphon off what may be applicable or appropriate for an individual's schedule. Sounds simple and routine, yet not so for those who have other agendas to communicate with their peers when they should be listening. Can you imagine the missed activities and appointments? Can you visualize the disruptions?

7

THE COPIER ROOM

Learning how to operate the copier machine properly is a must, whether or not one has advanced degrees. This friendly monster (an oxymoron to be sure) can be intimidating, but only to those who refuse to follow directions. Remember the old saying, "When all else fails, read the directions"? True, true, true. It has the appearance of a main frame with a tether, a lifeline, or possibly the teacher's umbilical cord!

Teachers line up throughout the day to pay homage to this machine. Lines, lines, and more lines—similar to the days of rationing, as if free-bees were the offering. I believe each teacher copies enough pages of materials every year to cover a thesis, if not a textbook.

The conversation before, during, and after this experience is indeed educational in itself. I wondered about my associates whose lessons for the next period or two depended upon their managing to photocopy materials just minutes before a class. This mechanical device could have an apoplectic fit at any moment, and then what happens to the prospective lesson? Beginning teachers beware: planning ahead is in the teacher bible.

Whenever I planned to operate the photocopier, I made sure I was never under any duress. In other words, if that monster of a machine failed to operate or those inevitable lines prevailed, I could simply take a walk, with the only loss being a few minutes of my time. This was not the case for several teachers who insisted on the immediate use of this appliance as though their lives depended on its use—and perhaps they did!

Remember the "keyword" (à la computer jargon) *organization*? Click on it metaphorically and let it spread across the entire screen. Or be the early bird—my son being the perfect example. He arrives at school at the crack of dawn (a slight exaggeration) to be the number one user. No line and the absence of any hassle. He realizes his trade-off: less slumber begets less stress, rather than more sleep causing more struggle.

I have never figured out how the photocopier knew that I was the operator! Whether early morning, midday, or afternoon, this apparatus became inoperable in my presence. It also saw fit to leave me messages on its miniscule prompter. Why, oh why, did I always seem to get a message that flashes *toner*? Why didn't the person before me or following me be the proud recipient of this message? Why me? Why the *add paper* message? How did that teacher before me make do? This scenario may sound ridiculous—but only if you are not the teacher embroiled in this scene.

I remember Carol, who had my schedule memorized and took full advantage of the situation. She often ran into this sanctuary in a panic, found me, appealed to my generosity, and with her display of persistence and sapience, obligated me to copy materials for her! Keep in mind that this woman was not one of my students, yet routinely managed to find me and cajole me to do these projects for her. Carol displayed such a sincere desire to work on these projects that I succumbed to her persistent persuasions; no, I was not naive. My only problem (for those moments), was "Why me?"!

By now it becomes apparent, once again, that the teacher wears many hats. The teacher is on call for all students, at all times, in all situations, in this remarkable plant. These are but a few of the reasons why every teacher has an influence on the majority of the student body, in and out of his or her own classroom.

8

THE COMPUTER ROOM

The computer room is another vital area where communication is the password. More often than not, one has much company while utilizing the computers and there exist ample opportunities for teachers to receive instructions in computer usage. It is always a good idea to take advantage of the various workshops offered. During these times (and others), the learning process continues.

Teachers schedule their classes in these environs to work on programs and projects covering a wide range of topics and virtually the entire educational spectrum. After all, computer usage is a part of the process of modern academic education.

Computer projects and research involve taking advantage of the Internet. Many students and teachers create their own websites, which can illustrate a topic and link to other related sites. Several communities around the country are integrating laptop computers into the classrooms where students pursue these projects.

Jake was the computer expert in one of my classes and he made this known throughout his class *and* several other classes. I took advantage of Jake's computer expertise and promoted him from student status to official assistant. It will become evident that I took advantage of this "assistant route." He helped me set up various programs and zero in on specific sites we intended to examine. This was indeed helpful with a class of about twenty students and two complete banks of computers—not an easy task for one teacher to manage.

This student seemed to thrive on his newfound opportunities and responsibilities until yours truly stepped in to interrupt his authority. I didn't mind Jake showing off his talents, but when he crossed the line and entered the control panel and changed the Internet access protocols, this was deemed abuse of his position. What was to be assistance turned out to be hindrance, and that was a no-no, as I explained to him.

This brings to mind that whether in school or at home, certain students must be monitored rather closely because a few are bent on logging onto inappropriate sites. We have this great technology to explore and learn, but it brings with it the bad and the ugly. I believe the Internet will soon be regulated. Allowing one's class to use the Internet involves additional concerns, awareness, and responsibilities that are brought to bear on the teacher.

By the way, Jake took his demotion in good spirits and I was relieved when he had only his computer to contend with. I'm not sure if he was trying to give me this message earlier but in the long run, my decision made both of us happier campers.

Students are also exposed to a wide range of activities: Hyperstudio (where multimedia displays are created), language and reading programs, math and science programs, English and social studies activities, special help programs, and physical education and art and music selections. Nonacademic programs exist just for fun, yet all such activities enhance the students' interests and proficiency with the computer. Most teachers take full advantage of the notorious e-mail facility and the capability of entering grades and comments into the computer.

In our school system, each teacher was assigned a single e-mail address and we were encouraged to use it. I must admit that I used the computer for occasional personal use, and I took advantage of the copier equipment for occasional personal use as well. (Perhaps after all this time, now that I've finally admitted it, my conscience will be clear.) I remember having to send the superintendent an e-mail (for the first time). I heard this unusual beeping and inquired what was happening, only to be told it was a busy signal—just like the telephone. I was indeed embarrassed, in spite of being a newcomer to this type of technology. Well, after repeated tries and the incessant busy signal, I gave up and personally hand-delivered my own message. This trip involved a total of about twelve minutes from building to building. Compare this to the total attempts with the e-mail of about six minutes duration (and to no avail). I could have saved a sufficient amount of time to visit the restroom! Eighteen minutes is a significant time block for teachers. I'm certainly not belittling e-mail, just appreciating the fact that some things never change. Teachers, like anyone else, must learn not to sweat the small stuff.

9

THE MEDIA CENTER

The media center houses a lot of audiovisual equipment that defies the imagination. Several schools have a control panel that enables students to coordinate and manage their own television productions. Many a student has become proficient manipulating sophisticated technical equipment under the watchful eye of the instructor.

There also exists much projection equipment, microphones and speaker systems, TVs with VCRs, CD equipment, digital camera capabilities, DVD equipment, master control panels, and systems that allow for state-of-the-art communication between classrooms within the school and classrooms in other schools in other communities via satellite. I realize not all communities have all of this equipment, especially the later technology; however, many school systems have some.

Several future actors, production managers, television consultants, producers, and directors' interests were spawned in such an environment. The media center is certainly a unique classroom where apparatus is the key word rather than a chalkboard/whiteboard type of mentality, yet one can find loads of fascinating dialogue, spoken and unspoken; it's a hands-on discipline, for sure!

Observing students producing their own videos was an education for me as well as the students. To see two students of mine, Stuart and

Leslie, being videotaped as they were conducting a newscast was enlightening. These two students seemed to be the most unlikely candidates to perform well before a camera, but that they did. Their rapport with each other and their demeanor was quite refreshing to witness. The most significant aspect of this scenario is the fact that these two youngsters, exposed to this alternative setting, conducted themselves quite differently than they did in the classroom. It was as if their personalities were transformed and alter egos emerged.

Students form opinions about teachers and subjects (now that's a revelation, I'm sure!) for many different reasons. Some are turned on by the teacher, some are turned on by the course, and some by both (it's referred to as ecstasy!). With Stuart and Leslie, I believe this type of environment was their forte. It was as though they were looking for a long lost course and, happening to find it, shrieked "Eureka!" I also believe they were fortunate to have studied with a dedicated, devoted, and talented teacher, whom I had the pleasure to know. I truly am not one for clichés that oversimplify circumstances, but if it were necessary for me to pick one cliché from the proverbial hat, it would be the "different strokes for different folks"—at least, as far as these two students were concerned.

Teachers take heed: try your best to visit other classes. Watch and observe your students in these classrooms. Watch and observe your colleagues in those classrooms as they teach. This is time consuming and, to be sure, tiring, yet the rewards will energize you to limits you never thought you would or could realize.

Don't be surprised if a student, without warning, positions a camcorder a few feet from your cranium, takes aim, and blurts out, "Teacher, I would like to know what you think about reviving the National Defense Education Act?" This will happen, and how you respond will make all the difference in the world to the questioner! It's not important how right or wrong your answer, it *is* important how you connect with the interviewer. In all fairness, there were also times when these students from the media center would approach the teacher and request an appointment for a more propitious time of the day.

Taisha had the ability to make such appointments with me, never give me any hint of her line of questioning, and use her skills to gently and methodically get me to respond about my teaching career. She made me think about situations that had long since left my gray matter. On one occasion, Taisha asked me if I was teaching the day President Kennedy was assassinated and if I was, what was the mood of the school. I was teaching that horrible day and I relayed the state of the school and frame of mind experienced by many of us. Keep in mind, the camera is rolling as one answers these all-important questions. Also remember that this was an assignment to be taped, brought back to the center, and analyzed for substance, clarity, projection technicalities, and all sorts of other criteria that were required for the course.

These assignments were always a pleasure for me to not only accommodate the students but to become involved with their academic lives. To see what else they were learning, aside from my discipline, was fascinating to me. I often expressed to students and faculty my wish that I could take the courses offered by my colleagues. Many would scoff and chuckle at the idea, but I reiterated that I was not making facetious statements.

Students from the media center are also called upon to videotape several schoolwide productions, such as plays, musicals, and guest speakers (remember those library events?), sports events, and of course, regular classes. This is an enormous responsibility because these videos are occasionally used to show the community what the school is all about.

The reader can tell that many of the interactions and communications from this chapter did not take place in "my" classroom but they did take place within the school. The teacher lives in the school and not in the schoolroom alone, analogous to "living" at home and "living" in all areas of the home.

2

"WITHIN" THE PLANT

10

MEETINGS

Faculty meetings are convened about twice a month and consist of discussions about a wide variety of issues (naturally). Some are devoted to routine as well as nonroutine matters. Are teachers making themselves visible or invisible in the corridors during passing times? If there is a hat/no-hat rule, is it being enforced? Teachers are also reminded of their arrival and departure schedules. Usually, there are also several other "reminders" of responsibilities, including handbook rules and regulations. These meetings are often more like a therapy session and serve as a sounding board to give the staff the opportunity to express opinions about gum chewing, the speaker system, corridor passes, or access to telephones. Discussions ensue about bells or no bells, backpacks, no backpacks, or "see-through" packs and their weight limitations. All sorts of discussions ensue regarding various alternative scheduling logistics for students and teachers.

With about thirty-six weeks of school, at least seventy to seventy-five different issues affect the teachers' daily lives in this complicated plant. When teachers meet to discuss, that means exactly that: discuss and discuss. Conclusions and decisions are not so readily apparent or forthcoming.

Teacher workshops are scheduled throughout the year, sometimes necessitating early release days for students. Workshops may include a wide range of topics to "keep the teacher well informed": child abuse, racism, left brain/right brain info, alcohol use and abuse, other drug education, new/latest teaching methods, interpersonal relationships, sensitivity training, the latest technology training, and at times, guest speakers. All these are intended to enhance one's ability to work at educating and many agree that at least the free snacks are well worth the time involved.

Teachers must be sensitive to all these issues, regardless of their teaching day. In other words, one is required to be alert and responsive to delicate matters at these sessions in spite of a day that may have begun several hours earlier with a parent or administrative conference. It is not uncommon for a teacher to feel as though classes were sandwiched between the meetings!

Some people deem meetings as an opportunity to catch up on some "shut-eye," correct papers, or gossip. These teachers are the ones who will miss a few details and foul up the machinery that the meeting was to help run smoothly.

In many districts, citywide meetings are held either once or twice a month. Teachers must attend the appropriate subject matter meeting, as these are intended to brief all teachers from all schools in the city. The curriculum and the methods of presenting the curriculum are discussed along with the various expectations of the coordinators. Announcements for workshops and conferences (local and national), supplies (permanent and consumable), and other budget matters are reviewed. This can be a harrowing time when teachers discover that what they need and what they will receive do not coincide. Yet, lest we forget, this is another good source of food! With many of these meetings on weekdays, built into the systems schedule, the teacher can forgo packing snacks for this day of the week. I always thought that the refreshments were the carrots that got us there and kept us in check(mate?).

Departmental meetings, also once a month and often during the school day, are held to ensure that everyone in the department knew what features needed addressing because it was necessary at times for all to be on the "same page" at the same time. I'm not sure where or when the "mental" part (of depart-mental) enters the discussions, however; the department does meet and these meetings can be productive. I believe it is important for each teacher to be aware of his colleagues' curriculum for obvious reasons (a thought not always shared by others).

The more the department members are informed, the better the efficiency quotient; this brings us to what is known as professionalism.

Team meetings are a conglomeration of team business, curriculum discussions, specialists, guidance personnel, administrators, and other pleasantries. Team business is certainly a mixture of many details that, if managed properly, enable the team to run smoothly—sort of synchronizing our watches. Some examples are the handling of progress reports (who receives them and when), field trips, finances, destinations, bulletins, individual student problems, behavior, achievement, assemblies, joint activities within the school, and various reports for parents and administration. Many such details are essential for a smooth running team. It is a blessing when members of the team see fit to work together for the mutual benefit of the team. This is another situation where interpersonal relationships are vital and scholastic degrees not so vital. When each teacher works for the good of the team, they have a winning combination. Not much different from any sports team working together—except, perhaps, for the salary differences!

Parent-teacher meetings are probably one of the most important avenues of communication. There is nothing new in the notion that parents must take an active role in the education of their children and working with parents is another important skill that needs to be nurtured. I would rank these meetings, whether individual (private) or group, at the top of my list when efficiency and success are crucial to the educational process. These conferences involve all sorts of human emotions, running the gamut from a variety of pleasantries, trivialities, routine, complicated, sensitive, delicate, sweet, and honorable issues and attitudes to unpleasant, belligerent, onerous, and disastrous ones.

At one meeting, one of the parents, Dr. Reynolds, proposed a deal as we met to discuss his son's fair academic standing. Sean found it difficult to live up to his father's expectations. He was trying his best; he was expending loads of energy trying to please his dad, but all to no avail and this, of course, precipitated the conference. Mrs. Reynolds fully understood her son's academic limitations and was pleased with Sean's all-around experiences in school. He played on two sports teams while competing for a part in the play and he was a class officer.

I pleaded with his father to be more tolerant of his son, to recognize his accomplishments, and to accentuate the positive: Sean was a contented adolescent. I tried to show Dr. Reynolds that this was his problem, not Sean's. A difficult assignment, for sure, and I was not about to relent. This bright (?) parent who had achieved much academic success in his own right could not understand or accept the fact that his son was not on the honor roll. It didn't matter to him what other talents were demonstrated by Sean; this father was totally oblivious to his son's super attitude, his sweet nature (especially for an adolescent), and his value system, which was tops in my book!

From the doctor came this proposal: "If you give my son a B this term, I promise you he will attain a B average next term!" My initial reaction was shock. Did I hear correctly what was being asked of me? Next, I felt I was insulted and demeaned; talk about total lack of respect! I also believed that Dr. Reynolds was trying to intimidate me and take advantage of my youthful appearance. (This experience occurred prior to nature truly taking its course; that is, I was endowed with substantial "cranial hair" of the brown variety. It is entirely possible this scenario might never have occurred had there been ten plus years on me. Or is it entirely possible this would not have made any difference? Leopards still do not change their spots.) I told the doctor that I got his message but that he didn't hear my message. Our entire dialogue apparently passed through his skull like a wind through the leaves.

Prior to my terminating this meeting, I wanted him to realize that he both disappointed me and his family and scared me with such subterfuge. Could he be a credit to his profession? Does he practice medicine with this sort of attitude? If so, we are all in for trouble. This was the final communication between Dr. Reynolds and me. There was never another communication from any family member for the remainder of the year—one sad commentary, and a very disheartening conference that left me thinking about it for several days thereafter. At least I now realized, even more so, what a remarkable youngster I was working with. Sean was making positive strides while his father was continually backpedaling. No need to feel sorry for this kid, he will continue to live a meaningful, rewarding life; I'm not so sure about his father.

There are situations where no rules, regulations, or directions exist. Trust in one's own good judgment and right will surely surface. If teachers are honest with themselves and their community, their sincerity and dedication will overcome most obstacles.

I am reminded of a conference with a parent whose son was "misunderstood." (Sound familiar?) Felix was a handsome, articulate youngster who didn't exactly place school as number one on his priority list. He knew what was expected of him, yet insisted on managing his own life without much interference from others. He was reluctant to adhere to school rules and diverted all attempts to put him on the correct track.

Several of my associates lost patience with Felix early on and "fought back" at the slightest provocation. The more he antagonized his teachers, the more resentment was fostered on both sides. The more resentment he felt, the more he became disinterested and remote, and a vicious cycle was perpetuated. I actually took my cue from observing his reaction to authority. This boy just did not like to be told what to do and when to do it! However, if I mentioned a task and left a message (verbal/written) stating how it could be accomplished, and with no deadlines, Felix cooperated.

We held a productive conference with Felix where all of his teachers, the guidance counselor, and his parent were able to articulate their concerns and come to conclusions that included realistic expectations. For example: Felix will respond to directions where alternatives are provided (sort of including him in the decision-making process). When situations arose that necessitated following directions, where no alternatives were possible, he was to respond with respect and do his utmost to be patient. This involved much practice; however, such "restraint" is part of the growing-up process that the teaching staff aims to foster.

Many complex issues were involved, including his attempts at identifying what sort of relationships he wished to pursue and with whom. Hence, we initiated a schedule of appointments with his guidance counselor. His acceptance of this approach and the various conditions arranged for on his behalf were important steps in the right direction.

This example, similar to several others, emphasizes the precepts and teachings we try to accomplish as we "intervene" in the lives of these youngsters. Much of my learning stems from getting involved in the personal lives of my students. I cannot imagine teaching without this personal communication.

Again and again, one can appreciate the teaching and learning that take place within "the plant" but not necessarily within "the classroom." This situation also demonstrates that students differ in the manner in which they choose to learn and respond to authority. This responding to authority and the ability to focus on certain tasks often complement each other.

Although some students are self-starters, some need a slight nudge, some need much motivation, and others require much more monitoring. In the final analysis, the teacher will naturally respond to all problems *and mistakes will be made*; however, opportunities abound for rectifications on subsequent days—the beauty of teaching.

It is always difficult to work with students who have experienced the loss of a parent or guardian. Candice, her twin sister Camille, and younger brother Rowland lost their mother to cancer and suddenly these two young ladies became young adults. They assumed responsibilities that normally would not have been heaped upon them at this "tender" age. Rowland, nearly ten years their junior, was not totally aware of the changes that occurred in his family and was certainly unaware of other ramifications. Mr. Torres, always the devoted, concerned, loving father, was himself thrust into this terrible situation. His initial reaction was the concern for his children, hence a call and subsequent visit with the teachers.

We, as teachers (and parents), tried our best to understand the circumstances and ameliorate aspects of their school lives. Mr. Torres displayed keen insight as he expressed his desire for us to assist his girls through this period of their life, without amplifying the concessions we were about to put into place.

I believe these two young women inherited, to a great extent, their father's level-headed disposition. I greatly admired the poise that Candace and Camille presented as they continued to excel with their lessons and at the same time maintain a sense of order in their home. They chose to be the primary caretakers of their young brother. Their afternoons and evenings were consumed with an amalgam of chores.

Words alone could not express how much I respect, applaud, and commend their father because I realized he worked hard to achieve a semblance of stability in his home. After nearly two months, this man believed the burdens placed upon his girls were counterproductive. Therefore, he shifted gears and insisted they slowly and gradually resume some of their former extracurricular activities, a wise decision.

I can't help but feel sorrow for my students and their families at times like this, yet I believe their resilience is remarkable, their love for each other is bountiful, and their support group is fantastic. Many students realize their teacher has love, devotion, and patience for them. Their teacher is a huge part of that support group, a fact that enables them to carry on with their lives.

A teacher is always teaching, whether or not a class is present. A good teacher realizes that these "contacts" are an integral part of the profession. The responsibilities are enormous, the details are mind-boggling, and the time invested is invaluable; at the same time, the energies expended are draining both physically and mentally. There is no "overtime" or "time and a half" for weekends or holidays, just that dedication, commitment, and sincerity I wrote about earlier. Many hours are involved, not just the proverbial 9:00 A.M. to 3:00 P.M., in planning, discussing, and devising the best methods and techniques to ensure the best possible education for *each* student. To create an atmosphere that brings out the best in each individual is extremely difficult and extremely rewarding for both the student and the teacher. Forgive me if I reiterate the previous sentence throughout this book!

I liken many of these meetings to an artist creating a masterpiece. The correct combination of teachers working together is a work of art. I believe the efficiency of the team is in direct proportion to the accomplishments the students will achieve and, ultimately, their successful school experience.

⓫

COACHING

Coaching is one of the activities and responsibilities I referred to earlier when I mentioned that teaching takes place in and out of the classroom. Team meetings take place in order to facilitate communication (what else!) between players and coach.

The coach must spell out the responsibilities each player has to himself or herself and to the team. Will a player commit to daily practice sessions that begin promptly at the close of school? When the game schedule is presented, are there any obstacles? If the schedules change, are the team members flexible enough to adjust accordingly? Does academic standing have any bearing on the team member's eligibility? In other words, is it necessary for one to maintain a "good" academic record to be considered for the team?

I always maintained that studies came first, yet if students wished to play and study, they were welcome to do so. Of course, there are always exceptions and these are the students and situations who create the ulcers: exceptions to academics, exceptions to attending practices, and exceptions to attending the games. It is therefore quite obvious that exceptions become the rule! Inevitably, there are also the ensuing parental discussions revolving around these rules. I believe not much can be taken for granted when working (living) with players and students. As the proverb states, "To be on the safe side, spell it out." And whenever there is dialogue and a presence with young adults, much time, energy, and patience is involved.

There are also "discussions" among the coaches to clarify scheduling and changes to schedules, to adjust for player alternatives, to reiterate certain rules and regulations, and certainly to listen to the myriad comments (mostly complaints) from the players (or prima donnas).

Coaches often take on the role of surrogate parents, which means they take the flak that goes with the coaching or parenting. Some ground rules are established as lineups are adjusted before the actual competition. This becomes an education for the coach because much strategy is espoused. One would think the war games are on and "prepare for battle" becomes the cry!

The games (or matches) can be construed as an ultimate kind of success as the coach tries to field a team from a conglomeration of many levels of ability and a variety of attitudes! Coaches must always be cognizant of the fact that these young people are just that. They are not the professionals that they believe they are and their egos must be considered. Who said coaching was all fun and games? (Pun intended!)

Practice sessions can be fun and indeed challenging for the coach and the players. Practice means just that: trying to improve upon your playing without a killer mentality and hopefully becoming an asset to the team and at the same time learning what sportsmanship is all about.

Awards always help with self-esteem, confidence, camaraderie, and a sense of accomplishment for an activity well done. The pride one has is truly a feeling of excitement and exhilaration. The award is a sort of culmination of a monumental goal, whether as a contributor, a helper, a sportsman, a winner, or a loser. This is not easy for many a youngster to learn; however, learn they must with the help and guidance of the coach. These are the rewards from coaching students. It is certainly not easy to expect a team to recognize "that was a good game" or that we did our best and played hard, yet still lost the game. Many a learning situation does not come easily.

I'm not sure these aspects were discussed in the preparation to teach; however, there is the proverbial "on the job training" that is ever present in the life of the teacher.

⑫

FACULTY AND STAFF

The faculty (teachers) and staff (administration) are a dedicated group of professionals who deserve much credit. I had the good fortune to work with colleagues, the majority of whom were well trained, sensitive, caring, and committed to their profession. I always admired and appreciated the vast array of expertise of a staff that was able to bring so much savvy and order to this complex plant.

Classroom teachers are the foundation of the plant. The enormous responsibility is truly mind-boggling. I believe the teacher is constantly on call, whether in or out of the confines of the school. I liken the feeling to an actor who is on stage during every act, in front of a live audience with the spotlight aimed, while some guests talk in the midst of the performance and others listen intently while the actor creates an impromptu speech from prepared notes. To be physically and mentally prepared for the inevitable repeat performance, at times with different scripts, each succeeding day is an incredible feat for the teaching *Homo sapiens*! A slight take-off on President Harry S. Truman's words is, "This is one place where the buck stops!"

So many negative comments are aimed at the teacher. I often felt that criticisms were the one constant with which a teacher lived. That old adage that it is impossible to please everyone all the time should be on a marquis at the entrance to the school. I would frequently be involved in some lesson and interject to the class that I (we) aim to please, therefore be patient with yours truly. Was this a humbling gesture? In my case, no way. I always meant what I said—or preached, as some of my students would say.

I always believed that all my efforts in working with the students were honest and sincere. Nothing, therefore, could deter me from my objectives. I was forever focused on trying to enable each student to achieve a successful school experience. Looking back, I'm not so sure I even batted in the proximity of the 80 to 90 percent range; however, the fact that I tried repeatedly continued to give me more impetus to succeed. Those nonproductive deeds and comments could not distract me from my goals.

I suppose that proverbial "thick skin" was really *my* perseverance and I hope the beginning teacher will develop her own defense/offense mechanism. I, however, had the advantage of the Rosenthal family motto: *labore, patientia, perseverantia!*

Guidance counselors are the teachers who try their best to serve as surrogate parents, clergy, and in many respects, friend. They are overworked and, at times, they are sounding boards for youngsters; at other times, they are models of understanding, empathy, and sympathy. They must be efficient mediators, negotiators, and givers of counsel—no simple task, especially when trying to communicate with several youngsters on a personal level.

Earlier in my career, I believed the guidance counselor's role was, in part, to enhance the communication between home and school, sort of an "addition to" syndrome. Later on, I realized that this professional had inherited the role "in place of" and that this had become the norm. With approximately a 50-percent divorce rate among adults, the prevalence of the single-parent home is most evident and this is where and why the guidance counselor most often enters the scene—in place of the missing parent. The education of the counselor has expanded to training (in cooperation with the classroom teacher) in areas of drugs, alcohol, smoking, suicide, child abuse, tolerance, divorce, peer mediation techniques, and testing, to mention a few.

A vast array of professionals specializes in dealing with students who have been diagnosed with learning disabilities: hearing impaired, speech and language disabilities, attention deficit disorders, and problems reading. ESL (English as a second language) teachers specialize in students for whom English is not their native language. It is certainly vital that all disciplines be considered in the decision-making process regarding a student's progress or lack thereof. Again, this is additional information that must be factored into the equation to allow the student to progress as best as he can.

As in any prescription for action, we must examine the possibility of the presence of any physical deficiency prior to examining certain emotional anomalies, and for this we have our most cherished school nurses. These nurses (usually women) have loads of responsibilities, from listening to tall tales such as sprained eyelashes, "testitis" (because next period is a test), self-induced fevers, and so forth to the more legitimate complaints. The nurse authenticates and documents all sorts of ailments and makes many difficult decisions. Medical records must be examined for certain illnesses, facts that will be relayed to the appropriate staff members. Physical exams must be arranged for with a physician if a student is to participate in various school sports. Yes, even nonscience teachers will be exposed to some anatomy and physiology and how this often relates to human behavior patterns. For every student with a problem, the entire team of teachers encompassing all disciplines will be briefed and a plan of action developed.

Same process in medicine: tests are performed and analyzed, a diagnosis is proposed based on these facts, and a plan of action is undertaken. The team of teachers and specialists follows through on certain proposals utilizing all sorts of techniques, many of which require training and practicing with not much room for errors.

This is an excellent example of the "team approach" to a problem, whether minute or not. As we all know, small problems spread, if left unchecked, into bigger problems. To witness positive results when the team "clicks" is gratifying. To make meaningful attempts to encourage a student to achieve and feel proud of herself is a difficult task for the teacher. We realize that we cannot always be 100 percent sure that we made the correct decisions. (Bells are ringing at this time, I'm sure, for the parents out there!) Nevertheless, teachers invest much time and effort working through pleasant as well as unpleasant situations that are inevitable in the students' lives.

Administrators are available to facilitate much of the logistics involved in scheduling and communications throughout the entire building. Their job descriptions are discussed in a separate chapter, for I believe this is another desk where "the buck stops," as put so aptly by Harry S. This alone might hint as to the complexity of the responsibility!

These "magicians" are the oil that keeps the gears shifting so smoothly. They are the cement that keeps the foundation intact. They are the generals on the front line ("firing line"?) who help give direction and a purpose to the plant. These wonders could teach courses on communication, economics, and political science, and simultaneously lead the parade of ambassadors.

Teachers communicate with many professionals and nonprofessionals, each deserving the same consideration of time, patience, and understanding. At times, such meetings may preempt a lesson or two. This refers to the fact that no teacher's world is limited to the classroom. I have made an attempt to point out an array, by no means inclusive, of experiences and encounters to emphasize the above.

At this point, I would also wish to mention that in *no way* am I trying to discourage teachers and potential teachers. On the contrary! I am bent on *encouraging* them. Again and again, I simply feel it is important for the teacher, as he is introduced to teaching, to be exposed to many of the complexities early in this multifaceted profession.

13

PARENTS AND GUARDIANS

Parents are often the lifelines for their students and certainly important partners in this process of education. The parent or guardian is the ultimate partner with the teacher if the student is to have a pleasant, memorable, and successful school experience.

Concerned parents and guardians who monitor their families and get involved with the school communities reap what they have sown, without a doubt. From my own experiences, friends' experiences, and even the experiences I can recall growing up, there was this kinship with the schools, maybe not a physical contact with the schools, but a genuine interest in all school-related activities. I remember a demonstrable interest if a student was "detained" by a teacher or anyone in authority. Any infraction of the rules was taken seriously by parents and these "lapses of memory" (as I refer to them) were not apt to be repeated. In my earlier years of teaching, I learned to spell out the behavior problem to parents with some sort of soft "backpedaling." I figured out that if I came on too vehemently to convince these adults that something must change, I might possibly not see this student for some time! In some households, there was such a no-nonsense approach that I didn't exactly want the student to disappear from terra firma!

Over time, rules and regulations at home were ignored and there prevailed a definite lack of consequences. Obviously, with the diminished controls on the home front, the teachers lacked this all-important dimension and there was a total breakdown in the continuity between home and school.

To further complicate matters, according to a recent survey by the Kaiser Family Foundation (a health research organization), many parents want schools to provide more sex education once their children reach their teen years. "They want discussions to include abstinence, birth control, STDs, abortion, and even sexual orientation." Nearly 66 percent of parents said such sex education should last at least half a semester or more and 54 percent said classes should not be coed. Eighty-four percent of the parents want explanations on how to obtain and use birth control available to the students.

"Parents want schools to tell students what to do if they are raped. Four out of five parents want discussions about abortion, and three out of four parents want discussions about homosexuality and sexual orientation."

Add these responsibilities to the already overloaded curriculum and the absence of the "home dimension," and we have teachers counting days until the end of the school year: not a healthy situation.

The following snapshot (from Yankelovich Partners for LearningPays. com) by Cindy Hall and Suzi Parker, *USA Today*, examines some additional statistics that shape our lives.

Parents spend an average of eight hours eighteen minutes per week with their children on their schoolwork or school-related activities.

Absentee parents and guardians amaze me because I'm forever asking myself "What are these people all about?" To have a child go though the school environs and not demonstrate a genuine concerted interest for their child's educational welfare puzzles me. I really do not wish to come across as the naive one, yet I find it difficult to reconcile.

These missing parents make the teacher's role increasingly difficult and frustrating. Without this consistent partnership (home and school), the student also has an added burden, a condition the student can ill afford. I spent many a day playing sleuth, and without a private investigator's license! I have tried to track down parents, like a modern Sherlock Holmes, and in several cases, to no avail.

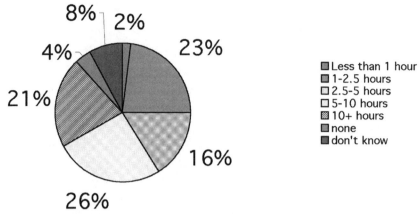

Figure 13.1   **Involved with education: time spent by parents.**

Most of us now communicate with a tape-recorded message on an answering machine or other electronic device. I refer to this type of communication as the "one-sided conversation." At least, there is no vociferous confrontation or, for that matter, no opportunity to discuss pleasantries with such one-way discussions.

Much vital dialogue takes place between parents and guardians and the teacher. Somehow, the beginning teacher must arrive at parent meetings equipped with some experience. Usually the on-the-job syndrome kicks in and the teacher hopes "and prays" he spoke appropriately (eloquence would be too much to hope for!) when it was his turn to speak. I am not poking fun but just commenting on the training for such delicate conversations!

Weekend parents/guardians are the occasional adults who every so often feel they are required to keep in touch with the school, sort of like former long-lost acquaintances who by chance bump into one another and pick up the conversation where they left off.

The teacher must accentuate the positive and take advantage of small blessings, one of which is that there must still remain that tether line from home to school, albeit only sporadic and tenuous. Some of these encounters via telephone, e-mail, voice mail, or snail mail might even include "weekend" communications but not necessarily. Sometimes a parent will satisfy the guilt, sometimes the parent will feel anger, and sometimes joy will abound. In every instance, though, I felt somewhat awkward and uncomfortable talking with a parent periodically instead of on a regular basis. This "timing" can and does put an additional strain on the communicators, and is certainly another difficult task for any teacher, and especially the beginning teacher.

I have loads of difficulty with what I refer to as the "split-parent syndrome." Some events included here can easily be interchanged with events in the chapter on students; however, the following "case" demonstrates how two parents can live together yet be living so far apart from each other!

I always looked forward to teaching Dawn. To witness the joy this young woman derived from her classes inspired me to try harder to assist her with her language and learning problems as they applied to her studies. Early on, Dawn had realized that much effort would be necessary for her to achieve minimal competency in most of her academics. Dawn refused to be denied a solid academic foundation. She had a positive attitude and great support on the home front of her brother and mother.

I shared her joy and never ceased to be amazed how her earlier haphazard struggles turned to more relaxed disciplined efforts. She was never reluctant to ask for help, she never shied from attempting new material, and she never complained while training and pacing herself to accomplish her goals. Dawn was indeed secure with her own agenda and thrived with the additional attention afforded her.

Much of this extra attention had its source in her loving and caring brother, two years her senior. A young man, who in his own right excelled in just about any activity he found to his liking, Dan understood his sister's needs and was perpetually willing to help her. His help was offered with a genuine love for her, wishing for Dawn to experience that sweet taste of success. Put more aptly by the one and only William Shakespeare, "Love sought is good, but given unsought is better."

Helping others was also the motto of this family. Mother and children were community-minded people who could be counted on to pick up the slack whenever a community project went awry. Dawn's mother was constantly monitoring her work and was the model parent as far as home-school communications were considered. Her demeanor was one of trust and cooperation as she worked with her daughter's teachers. This lady fully understood her daughter's limitations and this whole-hearted cooperation with the school made for a pleasant productive association.

At this point, as I'm sure the reader has noticed, there has been no mention of Dawn's father. He was a man totally divorced from school and "all therein," a successful, influential attorney with a professional schedule that demanded about eighty-five hours each week and loads of energy for his business interests. He had no hobbies, no resolution for relaxation, and time for his family was nonexistent. His wife was the type of person who reconciled "that was the way it was," and she accepted this dilemma as their way of life.

I believed this sensitive, devoted mother was perplexed with this situation and surrendered her feelings to the more aggressive behavior of her husband. What a tragedy to have his success measured only by his standards and his interests. This man could not reconcile the fact that his daughter lived with some disabilities that slowed and diminished her ability to grasp abstract concepts easily.

Most teachers realize they cannot control the destiny of the families with whom they come in contact, but they certainly have some influence. Inevitably, they experience some grief, some disappointment, and much pleasure.

Simply a slight diversion regarding "gifts" to end this chapter: The giving and receiving of them was frowned upon in my school. However, some parents and students were so appreciative, they insisted on rewarding a teacher with some small token.

For one example, Mrs. Green presented each teacher of her son's team (my team) with a finely crafted ballpoint pen with options for engraving them. Certainly, no teacher expects such "rewards" and teachers (at certain grade levels) are advised against their acceptance. Yet, depending upon the individual circumstance and the teachers' good judgment, it was wise to enjoy the gift and thank the givers.

Some gifts are given with the significance of various holidays in mind, while others are bestowed upon the teacher for contributing to the successful tenure of a student.

One contribution that made my day was when students sent CARE packages to various countries around the world in my name. Those gestures by no means minimized other generosities; however, the nature of the giving and the thoughtfulness expressed by students and parents was greatly appreciated. Above all, as you can tell, the gesture will be forever remembered.

⑭

STUDENTS

Students are the primary reason for the very existence of the teaching profession . . . and this book! I never like walking into a school that is not in session; it's too quiet and morbid and that's not natural. As soon as the students arrive, life is evident in the hallowed walkways and "normality" resumes. I have observed many classrooms that were so quiet that I closed my eyes for just a moment and felt lonely, as if the students were not taking tests but were temporarily absent from the room.

Middle school students (their name tag for now) in grades six through eight were the ones who occupied much of my time. I did teach in grades seven through nine (called junior high) for approximately twenty-five years from the '50s through the '80s, and high school students (grades nine through twelve) during the summer sessions for several years and in several different communities. College students were assigned to me for a project when I worked as a research assistant at Boston University Biological Research Laboratory in the 1950s. And I've been substituting in grades one through six during the school year of 2001–2002. So I've had a vast array of experiences working with students who spanned a spectrum from about six years of age to about twenty years of age.

Their abilities and character scales covered just about every known talent and disposition known to humanity. This was the fodder I thrived on, regardless of the anxieties and problems this "breed" presented. I suppose I never dwelled on the idea that I was burdened or that I was (definitely) exhausted or that I was harassed, although all of that did occur!

The Rise and Fall of the American Teenager by Thomas Hine has a chapter titled "Dangerous Adolescence." Mr. Hine notes that Granville Hall, the psychologist and founder of adolescent psychology, stated his "vision of adolescence as a beautiful and perilous time, and this vision still exerts a powerful influence over the way we see the young." Mr. Hall pioneered scientific inquiry into nearly every facet of the youthful mind and body and created persistent, destructive clichés.

I certainly agree that adolescence is a wonderful, fascinating, and perilous time, yet I hope I have steered clear of clichés in writing this book. I am weary of certain stereotypes and hackneyed phrases, especially when referring to the adolescent. These statements can and do confuse teachers, and can lead to misconceptions when trying to work with today's youth.

Most of the pleasures were mine, as I mentioned to my students; I hope some of the pleasure was theirs. I'm referring to pleasantries I experienced while teaching and how the students felt while learning (?). Even though there is never an easy moment working with youngsters—indeed, it is quite exhausting, as I've mentioned previously—working with them was the best part of my working day; it certainly could not compete with the innumerable meetings I was required to attend!

Even though the primary focus in schools should be on the students themselves, several "diversionary necessities" are inevitable. I cherished an old-time expression that served me well on several occasions: *tolerance for the ambiguous*. Teachers, old and new, need to be able to understand, appreciate, and have patience with unexpected events!

Now back to the students themselves. Many arrive carrying heavy burdens in addition to heavy texts, though some do travel light. These burdens range from serious problems at home to problems with their peers or with their teachers. There could exist an unpleasant divorce, illness, death, or signs of extreme anxiety and depression. Although there are assorted other specialists on location, it is usually the teacher who initially recognizes the problem and then brings this to the attention of the specialists and peers. The teacher's relationship with the student also might be a contributing factor to the well-being of the student. Indeed, there are enormous responsibilities for the teacher to be accountable and dependable in such delicate and important situations.

Several texts could be filled with a vast array of encounters; therefore, I have chosen some of the more significant (to me) and memorable experiences. These episodes are condensed in order to point out additional responsibilities added to the teachers' repertoire. Teachers are called upon to wear many hats and to wear them as though they fit to perfection. If the teacher wants to know what the good Lord looks like (and how the Lord would perform), this professional need only look in the mirror.

Several students left an impression on me, for better and for worse. Oh, so many memorable situations that gave me much pleasure! The pleasantries did not all come easily and there was a price to pay (at times) when I was learning. This learning went on for forty years since I wanted to learn, to teach, *and* to be a teacher. I believe that if I were to enter the starting gate a second time, I would opt for a repeat performance regardless of the different era. Naturally, names are altered to protect the innocent (or guilty?) in the following episodes.

Mike was a lonely eighth grader who was abused by his mother; the father was nonexistent. This chap became "street smart" as he roamed the streets many a day and night. When I finally did zero in on him, he became more withdrawn and extremely reticent to discuss any aspect of his life. I always approached him with great delicacy and had few opportunities to witness an underlying sensitive interior in spite of his rough-and-tough exterior manner. It was this interior I desperately tried to tap into and I made ever-so-slight inroads. When Mike didn't make the attendance roll call, I allowed him to enter the room (my/his homeroom) via "the window." This "entrance" was at ground level for a room that was below terra firma: a slight hop and jump and the torso enters. I'm not sure I realized how daring this move was on my part; however, there were times where I felt I needed to act surreptitiously and I seized the moment! These maneuvers put Mike and me on the same wavelength. Strange and unusual as it seemed, these encounters were the keys to unlocking this young man's psyche. He began to accept my goodwill gestures as sincere, and he trusted me. I understood his plight and he began to appreciate my responsibilities as his teacher; we began to develop an honest, caring relationship.

With this accomplished, my next task involved pursuing the inevitable academics. As he realized small and steady successes, a fact that enhanced his confidence, his world began to change and then he was, as said in thoroughbred parlance, "off to the races."

We met by accident several years later and, with nary a word spoken, our embrace said it all: what a reward . . . for us both! With head held high, chin protruding, chest outstretched, he proudly said, "Mr. R., I'm a chief machinist working for a reputable, top-notch company. I'm also happily married—to a former student of yours, Eileen!—and we are expecting our first child." Wow! This meeting not only made my day, it made my career!

Jack was the bully of the class and the grade. His physique was imposing for an eighth grader and his incessant growl-like demeanor enhanced his appearance. He used his brawn inappropriately and consequently his gray matter was left frozen in reverse—certainly an unhealthy state of mind to live with.

As his teacher, I pleaded with him "to count to ten" when this aggressive urge overcame his reason. I tried to communicate with his parents, who could not reconcile the need and urgency for additional professional intervention. Even our guidance staff extended themselves to the limit, all to no avail. Frustration continued on my part and I lived with the constant repetitious reminders to Jack to continue to work at some civility. Of course, I realized that I had a convoluted uphill road to climb as long as there was only minimal parental support.

My fledgling psychology skills continued to kick in and my meager experiences helped, but my ever-present gut feelings, empathy, tolerance, patience, and continued experiences working with students gave me a message of doom and gloom—certainly an uncomfortable feeling that I actually refused to submit to.

Years later, Jack visited me unexpectedly in school and I was flattered and quite pleased that he remembered our "experiences" together. The thrust of his conversation was his intent to become a state trooper. I observed a rather hidden agenda in his eyes, almost sinister, yet I tried to think positively. I always searched deeply into my soul to "observe" the eyes and "listen" to the diction and intonations. I could not see any empathy or a genuine willingness to help people in Jack's psyche, any more than I could when he was attending middle school.

I did assure him that I sincerely wished the best for him, hoped he made the academy, was successful, and that I looked forward to his return visit wearing his uniform following his graduation. In the end, Jack's dreams were cut short and so was his life. Nearly four weeks elapsed after we last met and I read an article in the newspaper that referred to Jack, who had been found dead from an apparent fracas. Drugs were scattered about the room and strong suspicions of a drug deal gone bad were expressed.

I thought long and hard about this young man and his family and I prayed that I learned much from such an episode, even though I was not fully prepared to deal with the situation. Yet I felt a sense of enormous relief and comfort that I had tried my utmost as Jack's teacher, advisor, confident, and friend.

With both Jack's and Mike's situations, there was no love or nurturing in the home, nor was there any sort of stimulation to learn. A caring, giving, sharing environment did not exist. Without this type of setting, the adolescent is ill prepared to face adulthood. It's routine for the adolescent to seek out peers and friends for advice on how to act and how to look and dress; however, we know that a sound beginning early in life allows the adolescent to grow with solid basic values.

Kristen was always forgetting her textbook, and I finally lost patience with her and blurted out, "How can I help you remember to bring your textbook to class?" I admit that I lost any semblance of tact and control and mentioned to my student teacher (at the time) that that was not how a teacher should have approached the subject. At least (or best), this student teacher realized that we do have a "human" side!

Later that day, Kristen came to my office and whispered that living with one parent for half the week and the other parent for half the week was confusing her, and that at times this schedule changed on a moment's notice! I apologized for my hasty rhetoric and gave Kristen my text. Now with two texts, she could leave one with each parent; I also made sure there was an "extra" for her in the classroom. Not an easy solution for me since the budget (barely) allowed for a single text per student. I had to make amends, enabling both of us to sleep nights!

Tom was one of my "star" tennis players for nearly three years. On the day of our final citywide championship match, he informed me just about two hours before playing time that he needed to skip the match and attend his Latin lesson (given by a tutor). I asked him if he realized how his decision would affect the team and he repeated his reason for not playing. I was quite disappointed with this decision and his remote attitude and demeanor. I immediately informed him of the consequences: immediate expulsion from the team roster, no "letter," and no mention of tennis on his "permanent record" card.

Within ten minutes, I was summoned to the principal's office to explain my decision. I held my ground and was relieved that the principal agreed with my decisions, although quite reluctantly!

This was a difficult and most unpleasant decision for me; however, I was focused more on Tom learning the meaning of commitment, dedication, loyalty, responsibility, and character than on the match. Even now, years later, I'm not sure if this experience was a benefit for this young man, but I know that the immediate needs of adolescents cannot always be tolerated, and one must take responsibility for one's actions. What a great time and place to learn this, early in life.

Another student, Allan, was bright, articulate, an excellent student, and a Boy Scout. We were working through the process of obtaining a merit badge in meteorology when I received a call from the main office wanting a certain important (aren't they all?) report immediately. This report had originally been due the following day; however, yours truly planned ahead—this time! Because I had left the report in my car, I asked Allan to retrieve it for me; his negative response was upsetting to me. Later that day, we talked and I came to the conclusion that this young man was not necessarily a credit to the Boy Scouts. I informed him of this and decided that he didn't merit the badge he sought. I had assumed Boy Scouts would help people in need, especially in emergencies.

Years later, a carpet was being installed in our den and at completion of the project a conversation ensued revealing that the installer was Allan's father! I relayed the story to him, adding that citizenship and character, as well as grades, were important dimensions in the learning process of the adolescent. In the end, my wife was pleased that at least I waited (by luck) to speak my piece until completion of the work! Allan's father did not care to allude to this past history. He simply stated that "Allan graduated from Harvard Business School and had a good job now." It was good to hear about such accomplishments; however, I was not convinced that his son's intellect matched his sincerity and kindness.

He may be a smart person, but is he endowed with some compassion, integrity, and character? Maybe time will tell.

As written in the *Ethics [Sayings] of the Fathers*, which embraces six centuries of Jewish wisdom and wit, "It's the me-first mentality that colors society's most popular road maps to success. True, intelligence is an indispensable tool to perfection, but unless it has a guiding philosophy it is like a powerful motor without a steering mechanism." I have taught many bright and brilliant students, students of average and not-so-average ability, but regardless of their intelligence, I tended to zero in on their moral character, their citizenship, their civility, and their ability to interact favorably with their peers and the adults who opted to devote their lives to helping them. For students to be productive citizens, I believe they must not lack these traits, for if they do, bright or not, they will be dismal failures in all endeavors. Have you ever met a student (or adult) who was very smart, but also quite evil? I have!

I will never forget one student, Susan. Several years later, she walked into my classroom unannounced, no warning, and entered as though a regular member of the class. Sue sat in the last row and listened (I think) intently and patiently to our discussion on drug abuse. I knew Sue had been involved with illicit drugs, was street smart, and her appearance seemed to coincide with that lifestyle. Her sudden appearance was a very apprehensive experience for me because I wondered whether I should elicit some opinions from her or ignore her presence during the class lesson. Not knowing Sue's frame of mind as she sat there actually confused and confounded me more so than annoyed me. I did have much trepidation about allowing her to elaborate on our discussions and I certainly wasn't sure how comfortable she would have been doing so. Would Sue have added much worthwhile "expertise," or would she have confused and relayed an inappropriate attitude? I opted to "play it safe" and talk with her following the class; at least I did not put her in a position to treat the topic with haste.

The look in her eyes gave me the impression she was experiencing an inner turmoil and returned to talk. Not necessarily to find answers, but to have someone listen to her. Oh, so much to comprehend for me and her and so little time; this was my biggest dilemma. We did talk, and talk, and talk, and I referred Susan to the most competent professionals I knew at the time that I believed could help. Years later, I discovered her life had abruptly ended. One of our school guidance counselors told me she had read in a local newspaper that Sue was found in a New York City motel room—cause of death: drug overdose.

My ever-present delight was to read about successes of my former students, never caring too much about what defined success beyond simply the honorable citizen contributing something to a community. I received much gratification as I learned about the good they spread. This served to reinforce my enthusiasm to continue helping them prepare for their future. Then again, I would read about those former students who went astray. Several had serious problems emotionally—problems with family (or lack thereof), problems in school, in their community, with substance abuse, and problems that covered the gamut of human emotions. These youngsters were always on my mind. Was there anything I (we) as their teacher could have done (or done differently) to intervene in their destructive path? Were the consequences they were exposed to fair and appropriate at the time? Did I give them the proper nurturing to define themselves? So many unanswerable queries that confounded and saddened me as I continued relentlessly to be a better teacher.

Early in my career, I wanted each and every student to succeed; if they didn't, I thought I had let them down. Of course, as the years flew by, I realized this was not the case. These adolescents and teenagers were immature and dependent and still required much guidance to help them with this period of experimentation and identity, seeking and learning. I suppose I let go of some of the idealistic school and societal principles and embraced more of the realistic school and society. I still wanted every student to succeed in his own way; however, I realized that in spite of my persistence, that was not to be and I learned to live with this feeling. I felt better for having made an attempt, rather than having made no attempt at all!

Included in my career was teaching science to students at a Hebrew academy (yeshiva), a difficult and rewarding experience for me, and one that I shall never forget. Difficult, from the point of view that teaching late afternoon and early evening was not the most conducive arrangement for teaching and learning. Rewarding, from the point of view that as a teacher I was afforded a different opportunity to teach.

This was a community of meager financial resources, which necessitated all sorts of varied strategies on my part for procuring funds and materials. I must add that I was not fully aware of, much less prepared for, all the ramifications involved with this venture. Soliciting materials and fundraising were not exactly in my realm and I often found myself begging and borrowing apparatus and certain paraphernalia. However, because such requests were in the name of education, this task was a bit more justifiable for me.

The particular lesson that I remember from the yeshiva was what I now refer to as the "crustacean caper." At the time, I was required to adhere to the Boston Public School's curriculum, a portion of which included the lessons on crustaceans. I thought that a great method to elaborate on this topic would (naturally) include "authentic specimens"—lobsters! A local market donated them, for the cause and in the name of science, and I was proud to be able to enhance this pending lesson. I will spare you the details of transporting and maintaining these creatures for our laboratory studies.

The day arrived and I began to prepare the specimens for study, including a laboratory guide and dissecting equipment. Within minutes, three of my students refused to work on these specimens. The unexpected response annoyed me. Their reasons had their origin in the Scriptures and they emphasized their beliefs by stating that it was forbidden for them to touch the lobsters. However, nothing at the time was going to deter me from pursuing this lesson, especially after what I had gone through to bring these creatures to the classroom. I invited the three students to leave the room and wait in the corridor until I had more time to discuss the matter. Instead, all three left the building! Remember I wrote about late afternoon/early evening sessions? Well, no administrator or any other adult was on the premises at that ungodly hour. I continued with the lesson, left the building in a state of confusion, and experienced a sleepless night.

When I bravely returned that next day, I was immediately summoned to the office of the executive director (a rabbi who had also been my teacher many years earlier) and listened carefully to a rather lengthy list of complaints. For the first time in my brief career, I felt as though this meeting was the preliminary to the firing squad. I was doomed, and maybe expected to turn in my Star of David pin! Rabbi R., whom I greatly respected, explained the problems I created for him, for the school, and for the entire community—and how his telephone had been ringing throughout that previous evening.

After much listening, I finally exercised what courage (?) remained and asked Rabbi R. to point out in the literature where it is stated that yeshiva students are not allowed to touch and study such specimens! The rabbi, being the learned and wise person that he was, realized that these students had their own (mis)interpretation of the law. Lobsters are certainly not on a list of kosher foods, and by the same token, the students were not being asked to include them in their diet! Therefore, we all concluded that working with the crustaceans was quite different from eating them!

This entire adventure raised an important point as far as I was concerned: Dogmatic attitudes can and do interfere with the learning process and can impede healthy progress—although years later, I received an invitation to attend the medical school graduation of these youngsters.

Ashley was a happy, contented, energetic, bright model in public school. I referred to her as the model in the class (not model of the class) because she displayed (ok, modeled) the latest fashions and, consequently, what the best-dressed student wore. She would ask me questions during the class discussions that had no bearing on what was being discussed. Nearly a full school week had elapsed before I realized that Ashley simply wanted the young men, and a few young women, to be aware of her presence. Wearing the latest fashions solidified this position, in her opinion. This bright, savvy girl also repeatedly followed a line of questioning that was definitely inappropriate to our lessons!

It was necessary for me to intercede with that type of behavior because the class could not afford such distractions. Ashley and I met and discussed how she could truly assist me and the class with more appropriate contributions, thereby displaying not only her apparel but also her appeal as the intelligent young woman she was. This constructive discussion put us both on the same wavelength with a favorable ending and a favorable beginning.

What I remember most about past students is just what I have been writing about. I can't always remember if Tom, Dick, Harry, Joan, Jane, Jill, or Jack were A or B or C students. I seem to remember whether they were good citizens (or not) in and out of school. One way of determining their good "citizenship" was to see how a class treated the substitute teacher. In my absence from the classroom, I expected (not quite demanded) all students to be respectful to whomever was trying to help them.

I always think highly of the substitute teacher (and not just because my wife and I currently work as substitutes!). To enter a domain that is unfamiliar much of the time and immediately take charge is a job for a general!

Teachers are required to have a "sub folder" on file, which includes the basics: emergency lesson plans, materials for carrying out the plans, the teacher's schedule of classes, time schedules, school map, and the name of a person who could assist with any questions.

There were students who were enthusiastic assisting a sub, and there were students who, on occasion, went in the opposite direction. By the time my sub folder was used, the majority of my students had a very good understanding of my expectations. The few instances where cooperation was not the "name of the game," I made sure students were held accountable.

One of my many duties was to administer first aid to students when and if an emergency occurred. In those early years of teaching, there was no full-time nurse on duty in the school. Have we not witnessed progress along these lines in education?! This was the one responsibility that I balked about, continued the plea for my removal from this capacity, and finally won the war after losing a few battles with the principal.

Prior to winning this conflict, it was mandatory for me to enroll and complete a certified first aid course. This requirement was taken in stride because I realized I could (and eventually did) utilize this knowledge as the tennis coach.

It became increasingly difficult for me to convince the principal that the very nature of my laboratory-oriented science classes made it impossible for me to respond adequately in an emergency. Again and again, I reiterated my position that if I should be in the midst of an experiment, a most likely situation, it would be most hazardous for my health and the health of others, to suddenly leave the class. Because no concrete provisions were provided for me along these lines, I was confronted with a terrible and potential disastrous situation. I casually informed my next-door colleague about my predicament and prearranged a "temporary" plan!

My battle cry ("No man can serve two masters at once") was ignored until a serious accident occurred in the industrial arts room when a student lost a section of a finger in a table saw accident!

I received the call for first aid assistance and within seconds I had turned off the gas jets, grabbed my first aid kit, opened my neighbor's door and shrieked "Watch my class!" made a beeline to the site of the accident, tended to the patient, and sent word to notify parents/guardians, police, and if time, the hospital. In this case, the police arrived within minutes and they set off for the hospital. I recovered a section of the finger, wrapped it in ice, handed it to the returning police, and eventually returned to my classroom. By this time, a different class inhabited the room. I must admit that I had lost track of time, day, period, and science lesson.

Would anyone question me when I tell them what a blessing it is to have the services of a full-time nurse on the premises? This episode was "the straw that broke the camel's back" or "the saw that took me aback!" It was the finale for EMT Rosenthal!

Teachers are routinely expected to "serve several masters simultaneously" and this brings to mind an article I read some years ago in a National Educational Association (NEA) paper. The title alone was intriguing: "Teachers Could Run U.S. Steel Corporation." I say, why not! They are organized, committed, and dedicated, have excellent communication skills, intelligent, considerate, compassionate, and patient, adhere to a budget, and make well-informed decisions. You are hired; when can you report to work? And for a pragmatic type of compensation!

The definition of the adolescent and the consequences of the onset of puberty has been and will continue to be apparent. Dr. Fred Streit writes about high school adolescents and "the major social world of the adolescent and how the peer group is a strong influence" at this particular time in their lives. I tend to believe that middle school students share some of these same characteristics. Oft times, these traits are highly individualistic and generalizations do not do justice to a discussion.

It has always been a most difficult task to communicate with grandparents about the rebellious and troubled adolescent who happens to be their grandson.

Zack's father was (is) an alcoholic who abandoned the family when Zack was about eight or nine years old. His mother suffered with severe depression, a condition that necessitated her confinement in a hospital, and this left Zack in the care of his grandparents, both between the ages of about seventy-four to seventy-eight. For fear of losing this youngster to the state, they chose to legally adopt him.

The immense physical and psychological changes that accompany adolescence are indeed difficult for any student residing in a functional, stable home. If there had been any stability in Zack's early life, he would certainly have had a better chance to cope with and survive these pressures; however, this was not his fate.

This young man came from an unstable environment, one certainly laden with strife. Positive influences were lacking, no parental love and nurturing were evident, and there was no stimulation to improve his mind. He was set up to be a destructive influence to himself and society. Zackary demanded extra attention from me, and that he received. When he tried his best to disturb and interrupt the class lessons, I insisted (demanded is probably more accurate) that he keep me company at the close of school for some tutelage.

Without delving deeply into all the specifics, I can write that we listened to each other's needs, discussed my responsibility to the class and to Zack, and pondered his responsibilities as a member of the class. I saved some of his past papers that I believe demonstrated accurate conclusions to previous class work. I tried to specifically point out why he should have been proud of himself and reinforced as best I could that he could be a contributor to the class. I believe he parted with a better understanding of "the rules" and the consequences that would be invoked if these rules were not adhered to.

Along came parents' visiting day, the time we teachers set aside for conferences, usually following the distribution of the infamous report cards. Zack's grandmother and grandfather joined me for a straightforward meeting. Grandmother immediately accused me of being too hard on him, while grandfather agreed with the slow but strict and steady progress I believed I was making. This was not an easy conference to conduct yet we all agreed to stay the course.

A few years later, while waiting to welcome my summer school students at the high school, a student by the name of Zackary entered rather sheepishly, somewhat embarrassed, and slithered into a seat (like many students do). Can you imagine firing neurons with impulses jumping the synapses at phenomenal speeds as we looked each other in the eye? I was elated to see him because the fact that Zack showed up told me he was on the correct path. We did have a successful summer experience and it was obvious to me that he worked hard on his studies but also worked hard on building constructive relationships. I told him how proud I was of his latest accomplishments and that I expected him to continue to make his grandparents proud of him. The telephone call from Zachary's grandparents that I received at the close of the summer session also helped make my summer successful.

Another year, another parent conference session. This time, I was confronted by two parents who wished to discuss the progress of two daughters. Nancy's father was living with Michelle's mother and both girls were living in this same household—a soap opera of the '90s. I stumbled through some general introductions before I could gain my composure. In any event, my initial inquiry was which girl was to be discussed first and obviously confidentiality was not an issue, right? Thank the dear Lord that these two girls were teachers' dreams, for this certainly ameliorated the discussions. They were a pleasure to teach, they wanted to learn, they were a credit to the school, and I began to feel a bit more at ease as I relayed this to the parents. I also had a gut feeling that this guardian/parental arrangement was of the fleeting variety; however, at this time, all parties seemed to be enjoying the honeymoon and the girls were thriving in school. That is all that mattered to me; the rest of the story was none of my business! Sometime later, my wife and I attended the Bat Mitzvah services and celebration of both girls.

I'm always honored to be included in various events in my students' lives and quite pleased to witness their diverse and extraordinary talents. Such occasions allowed me the perspective of not only sharing in their lives but also being part of a community. At times, I had ambivalent feelings about accepting invitations to attend personal or family events of my students, especially if they were current students. Parents were most kind and appreciative of the attention their children received and often wanted me to share in their joyous occasions. Therefore, once in a while, my wife and I would accept an invitation.

It's a given that most students in the middle school and the high school are loyal to their peers. They confide in each other and defend each other in spite of their awareness of wrongdoing. At times, I believe it's not so much a matter of aligning oneself with a friend as it is to join hands to oppose the teacher. That "common enemy" syndrome has some rhyme and reason for the student. Many are not willing to do the right thing, stand up for what they truly believe, and not be a mindless follower, regardless of "friends'" opinions. Sort of reminds me of the politician who says what he knows people want to hear rather than says and does what he actually knows is right, and not compromise his principles—for sure, not setting good examples.

I am reminded of the field trip to the science museum. These are the times where I am especially diligent, which is not an easy task when taking nearly one hundred students, several teachers, and a few parents on such trips. Teachers are well aware of the enormous responsibilities and details involved in taking on such excursions. Who is that person who said teachers have the day off?!

On leaving school by the proverbial bus transports, I noticed the boys at the rear sitting rather subdued, whispering, and nearly simulating the huddle of a football team. Two thoughts: I wondered if the early departure hour was the reason for their lack of activity, or whether they did not wish to call too much attention to themselves. I decided to give them "more rope."

The buses parked in a rather dark garage at the museum and once we checked in, touring time for the groups was in order. I continued to survey as much area as possible and I noticed a former student touring with some of us. Jim told me he was there with his mother. Although I doubted his sincerity, I congratulated him on his decision to visit this building and wished him a pleasant afternoon, especially in the company of his mother.

Boarding the bus for our return trip followed the same pattern with the same boys taking up the same positions as upon our arrival. Here they made another blunder as far as I was concerned. These guys were just too cool, especially after all that consumption of sugary food.

When the roll call was completed prior to departing, I began to move into position toward this sacred territory at the rear of the bus and announced that our bus could not and would not move until our head count was completed. I asked a few of the boys to stand and, lo and behold!, there was the stowaway beneath the seats curled up in a fetal position. I informed him that his departure from the bus was imminent and I expected him to comply with my wishes . . . if he wanted to avoid speaking with a police officer. Jim realized (smart fellow?) that there were no alternative options for him and he left the premises. I did offer a suggestion that possibly his mother could take him home, and I waved goodbye to him as we left the parking garage!

I accepted the fact that I would be tested, and it took time for me to understand the insults to my intelligence when students perpetrated such episodes. As the teacher learns and practices what is preached, these youngsters become savvy and begin to respect the teacher's experience. I remember a group of students telling me that I reminded them of Columbo! This television character was a police detective (lieutenant) played so aptly by the great actor, Peter Falk. This example surprised me because I didn't own a raincoat like the one Columbo wore, I didn't drive that old "jalopy" (close to it) that Columbo drove, I didn't smoke cigars like Columbo did, and I was not blessed with Columbo's good looks. The compliment, I hope, referred to Columbo's demeanor. He had a unique disposition and a behavior pattern that I admire. (No more of this, for fear of boasting and bragging; it's also embarrassing!)

Another example of this misplaced loyalty occurred when I offered to allow Lindsey, who was a member of another team (not one of my students) to join us on our weekend mountain trip. Unable to attend her team's trip due to family circumstances, we consented to make all the necessary arrangements, by no means an easy undertaking. All the rules for appropriate behavior were spelled out along with the remaining logistics. These logistics involved the pairings of roommates in the evening and what was expected of each student. At times, I felt like a camp counselor as I patrolled the dormitories assuring that all students were accounted for and all students were in their assigned rooms.

Unfortunately, Lindsey and some of her friends didn't comply with the rules and, to say the least, disappointed me as well as other teachers on the trip. I expected (naively) that Lindsey would demonstrate her appreciation and make that extra effort to cooperate with us. That was not the case and her uncooperative attitude caused me much grief. I informed her of my displeasure with her behavior, especially after I had devoted so much time *and* energy to see to it that she would not miss this super educational opportunity.

There is no rubric for determining consequences for her behavior and that of others; however, in the end, I made my feelings known to Lindsey's team teachers and parents and strongly suggested that she be denied the opportunity to join the entire grade on our end-of-the-year trip. This suggestion was upheld by all concerned parties; however, my main concern was that Lindsey learn a valuable lesson, especially where the consequences were not life threatening.

Students possess a sense of humor and, coupled with their sense of ingenuity, can create some funny (?) situations.

My beginning years of teaching seemed to invite several visitors to observe the classes. On one occasion, I informed my students of such a pending visit (mistake #1) and was counting on them to make a good impression (mistake #2); sound familiar? Naturally, I counted on the "know-it-alls" to strut their gray matter when called upon, similar to the peacock's showing off its plumage as it pranced about. Well, these bright, articulate students who *always* answered questions before I finished asking them, acted as if I had sedated them. My hopes and plans backfired and they succeeded in embarrassing me and creating an awkward situation!

I learned a lesson via this "fun and games": not to trust or depend on the "stars" of the class! A more important lesson for me involved much more consideration for other members of the class. Try to invite and encourage all students to participate, especially those who have continued to "burn the midnight oil" in order to succeed, those who have realized their newfound skills, those who have persevered in spite of much adversity, and those who have vastly improved their performance.

Another episode was perpetrated on yours truly, who to this very day continues to maintain a sense of humor, in spite of the "chromosome caper":

Andrew sat in the front row middle of my algebra class, worked conscientiously, made worthwhile contributions, was rather mature for an eighth grader, and was a pleasure to teach. Some days I would observe Andrew jogging past my classroom. No sooner had he passed by than I would notice him for a second time pass me heading in the opposite direction. All this movement seemed to be the routine flow of traffic, although it also seemed to me that he must have been rather confused as to where he needed to be. I had no reason to question his movements, however, until speaking with another team's teacher of the same grade. During the course of our conversations about students, Aaron's name surfaced along with some family background. The words *identical twins* were mentioned.

One must understand that as the school year commences, some teachers examine, without delay, the students' records. On the other hand, I was satisfied to discover various personalities as the school year progressed. When the words *identical twins* were uttered, immediately the bells rang, the buzzers buzzed; I received a message, and thank goodness, before it came to the hum of the sledge hammer! *The two boys I had seen in the hallway were not one and the same, but two and the same!*

I spoke with both boys and several amazing and interesting conversations and situations ensued. These two actually had much fun and pleasure at my expense as they switched classes on me. I was totally "clueless" (à la my daughter). Whenever Andrew or Aaron sat before me, they triggered my subtle sleuth mode: observe but do not stare, a difficult move. To me, this was the epitome of frustration for their similarities were so utterly identical, it was nearly frightening!

At no time could I guess with any sense of accuracy which youngster was present. I resorted to a few "tricks," but these generally entailed too many side effects and all to no avail. These guys knew they had their victim (teacher) "on his knees"; I succumbed, and they continued to play it for all its worth. All in all, this was just another experience in the life of a teacher where patience, prudence, finesse, and sense of humor are gateways to the teacher's success.

Another dimension of my teaching was in the realm of private tutoring: tutoring math, science, English, Bar and Bat Mitzvah lessons, and tennis. A few of these were more eventful or notable than most.

Tutoring tennis to Dan, a former math student, was a pleasure. The pleasure however, soon turned to displeasure. We started out with some of the basic handgrips after the proper size racquet was purchased and we headed off to the tennis courts. The pleasurable aspect was watching Dan improve and enjoying his newfound hobby. I also became the chauffeur for his lessons and eventually for the tournaments that I encouraged him to enter. Unfortunately, his parents were in absentia throughout all of our practice sessions in addition to his tournament play. This is where my displeasure entered. Speaking with his parents didn't seem to make a difference in their behavior pattern. Dan's parents were working at arduous and tedious professions to support him, his sister, and the upper-class lifestyle they were accustomed to living. They seemed to feel these "extras" more than made up for their absences.

Years later I met Dan's mother, by chance, and she lamented the fact that Dan never returned home following graduation from college. That is, he never wished to visit his parents or establish some sort of communication with them. I will always remember the expression on his mother's face when she said that her husband could not understand why his only son "cannot find the time" to visit him, "especially after all he had given him."

Earlier, I mentioned that I also tutored in English. Emily was my only English student, and I had loads of assistance from a master teacher. I was the teacher who needed tutoring, not only in the English curriculum but also in sign language. I was also made privy to the family's history of certain disabilities and was asked if this would deter me from helping this young girl. My mentors (I had many) seemed to think that my pronunciations and intonations were suited to Emily's style of learning since she did have ever-so-slight hearing and was an excellent lip reader.

Tutoring Emily became one of the best and most memorable experiences in my career: a science and math teacher teaching English to a legally deaf girl who was reading my lips and progressing by the proverbial leaps and bounds. This was indeed a humbling apprenticeship for me and one I looked forward to every day. Emily made my days; *she* allowed *me* to truly believe in myself! I often wondered who was teaching whom. This girl had much love, patience, and confidence to spread about. Nothing was ever taken for granted and the words *appreciate*, *respect*, and *love* were at the top of her vocabulary list. Of course, speech and language specialists are now present in many classrooms to assist learning disabled students.

Tutoring (teaching) curricula other than in my "fields of concentration" (sounds like college) added some trepidation to my psyche. It finally dawned on me that believing in oneself might reveal a hidden confidence. Specifically, my next self-imposed "assignment" was helping Rachel with her Bat Mitzvah lessons while simultaneously tutoring her in math. Her parents' anxieties were heightened as her big day was rapidly approaching. This wonderful milestone in her life involved much study and necessitated added responsibilities, and Rachel was finding it difficult to keep up with her secular studies and prepare for a Bat Mitzvah. Little did I realize that I would be carrying a skull cap (yarmulke) in my briefcase as I made the rounds—sort of "carry skull cap, will travel!"

Rachel was a pleasure to teach—not because she was a student who did everything to please the teacher, but because she was teachable. Open to all suggestions, willing (and able) to accept criticism, able to accept failure and move on, express ideas, form opinions, share them with other classmates, explore, explore, and explore, and think through intricate obstacles. My wife and I helped her celebrate her special day.

Teachers' cups overflow with special days and the majority of them occur in the classroom, and most assuredly within the confines of the plant.

Kishon's sudden and conspicuous absences led me to call home and learn that a family member had been in an automobile accident and succumbed. When I informed the class that Kishon's dog was killed by an automobile and that he was quite distraught over this, several of his classmates found the incident amusing. Specifically, members of his class found it difficult to believe that their "friend" could be so upset over the loss of his pet to be unable to return to class, but this was the case.

I asked if anyone had ever lost someone they loved. I asked if they did, how did they feel? I asked if anyone had a pet animal. I asked if their pet ever showed any affection toward them. I asked what attention they gave their pet. My intent was to get them thinking about others and not elaborate on the intricacies involved on the subject.

I mentioned that I felt it takes a mentally strong and kind, sensitive person to feel so attached to a pet. I relayed the fact that many religions of the world consider kindness to animals as a virtue and I remember my parents saying that persons who are kind to animals reveal their own tenderness. I also mentioned that I had enjoyed the company of two different dogs while growing up and felt sadness when their deaths did us part!

End of story, for it was up to some of Kishon's classmates to (re)think their own feelings and how they would react to others in similar situations.

My family is well aware of the fact that patience and nostalgia are my middle names—odd names, for sure! We've covered the patience; now for the nostalgia.

Passing the clothing store with the family name of my former student Rob, whom I had taught several years earlier, I could not resist stopping in. Unfortunately, Rob had died after a serious bout of pneumonia and all I could do was relay to his father how I remembered him. Rob was the quiet, skeptical loner of the family; to say he was shy was an understatement, yet when approached, he was readily willing to respond. In other words, I had realized I must go to Rob if we were to build a relationship. He accepted my suggestions to improve his academics while insisting on traveling about school with a briefcase, so much so that this briefcase became a trademark of his. Picture the rather slight frame of an adolescent shouldering an oversized briefcase. Today, this bag would be of the transparent variety, out of necessity!

After our relationship was on sound footing, I referred to him as "double o seven" (007). His entire demeanor—his expression, appearance, and mannerisms—all fit the sleuth image of James Bond! Allowing me to tag him in this manner was my "foot in the door." As the months passed, his skeptical nature seemed to diminish, he made some friends, and I believe he thrived at the mere calls of double o seven! "Double o seven, how are you?" "Can we study together?" "I need your help with this math problem, double o; what are you doing after school today?"

Double o seven was an asset to the class. He became willing to contribute to class activities and willing to part with some of his ideas. He found his niche and a comfortable one at that. He seemed to abandon his reticence to communicate with his peers, yet was especially discerning in choosing his friends.

If it's inherent in a personality to be "on the quiet side," so be it. The teacher, together with other professionals on the staff, will eventually determine causes for behavior patterns and then proceed with a course of action. Again, the challenges the students present appear in a variety of shapes and sizes; how the teacher lives with these challenges makes for this rewarding career.

I refer to the following as the "serendipity episode." Hanna was not a student in any of my classes, but she was a member of the homeroom. Two months into the school year, I was working intently with a student, looked up, and asked Hanna the time. Homeroom period is of a brief duration and I try to take best advantage of this valuable time. No response from Hanna as she signed out to the ladies' room abruptly. I didn't give much thought to this situation until on another occasion I asked Hanna to assist me with filling in various activities on our school calendar. At this time, I observed hesitations on her part when the dates, times, and months were to be considered. I concluded that Hanna did not know the months of the year in any sequence, nor could she tell time! This was not the time to exhibit any sort of surprise or bewilderment; however, I was shocked that this sweet girl made it to the seventh grade without these basic skills! And no mention of the sort in any records.

Our subsequent tutoring sessions were pleasant and low key, yet progress, progress, and continued progress were the keywords as we logged on to the situation and toyed with our homemade clock. The equation "practice + patience = progress" was working even as we toiled with the calendar and additional numbers. These were Hanna's lessons, this was Hanna's life, and I was relentless with her as I insisted our goals would be attained.

Initially, I spoke only with Hanna's mother (a single parent) to articulate my thoughts and ideas, and subsequently, two of her teachers agreed to allow me to substitute my lessons for her regular scheduled math and science lessons, thereby enabling me to pursue my plan. This young woman was to learn these basics and no alternatives were to be offered.

With much dedication and some frustration on Hanna's part, she succeeded and was commended and rewarded for her perseverance. Remember the Rosenthal motto: labore, patientia, *perseverantia*! What a pleasure to witness such determination and ultimately witness a character makeover. Hanna was proud of herself and to me that was success at its best. Elie Wiesel, author of *And the Sea Is Never Full: Memoirs 1969*, would have relished this encounter, an unusual situation and the "awakening of knowledge . . . unique light of understanding. . . . What a beautiful moment."

These are the experiences that teachers cherish. My battle cry (to my wife) continues to be, "You win some, you lose some"! Although the "some lost" continue to disturb me, the "some won" have more than compensated.

Rebecca was totally devoted to (or maybe consumed by) school. There existed an obsession with grades and no other aspect of school interested her! This girl was mirroring her mother's idea of what experiences were most important for her in school: "maintain an excellent academic standing and leave with an excellent academic record and I will be satisfied."

Rebecca was *never* allowed to pursue her own interests and *never* allowed to exercise her own options; therefore, any and all accomplishments in this realm of academia were in the name of mother. I could set my watch by this girl. To homeroom on time, promptly a beeline to her seat, immediately her nose to the text. Like a runner off the starting block when the go sign was given, so went Rebecca from class to class and from school to home. Her life was devoid of any extracurricular activities, including associations with classmates and other acquaintances.

I remember asking a particular question on an exam that required explaining various stages in the process of cell division (mitosis). As I read Rebecca's answer, I felt as though I were listening to an echo. Her words were carbon copies (or in today's parlance, "Xerox," laser printer quality): copies of my diction, spoken in class, down to the prepositions! Naturally, her answer "matched" the question perfectly, almost to the point that I thought she was teaching the lesson! Of course, her perfect score was . . . perfect!

Approximately a month later, final exam schedules were posted and my exam included a question on this identical topic. I opted to adopt a single portion of my previous question. Basically, I asked for an explanation of one stage of the entire cell division process: students were to elaborate on one specific section rather than the entire sequence. Apparently, taking this stage out of sequence was too much for Rebecca to process. This move upset her "strict memorization pattern" and consequently her answer to the question was far afield! This was a classical example of studying for *one* exam only, with no intent on understanding, and a travesty in Rebecca's education! Couple this with the mother's distorted vision for her daughter's well-being, and I could see that loads of work lay ahead for all parties.

At this stage in the story, I expected and received a telephone call from the mother requesting a meeting for an explanation for Rebecca's not-so-perfect exam grade. During our meeting, the mother behaved in her usual uncooperative manner and all forms of reason eluded her. This pathetic woman ignored my attempts at explanations. I searched deeply into my own mind to make intelligible the entire situation. I tried to interpret, to bring out meanings not immediately apparent (according to the *New World Dictionary*), to be cautious, patient, sympathetic and yes, even understanding, all to no avail. An unpleasant yet necessary meeting that I thought would be somewhat productive; however, loads of work continued to lie ahead.

When I would think of what lies ahead, former students came to mind. Would we ever meet or speak with one another again? How are they managing their lives? To what extent did they further their education? Where do they live and what are their occupations? Are they married, with a family? Writing about how former students are living their lives conjures up, in particular, that notion of meeting once again.

Teachers will inevitably meet and greet students, current and former, in almost any environment. Be prepared or simply be yourself and get accustomed to this. These encounters will most likely be pleasurable.

My wife was very patient and a good sport as we tracked through a section of the Florida Everglades during our February vacation, swatting mosquitoes and taking pictures of alligator families.

Finally, exiting the swamp and brush area, off the beaten track, I heard a voice off in the distance, sounding somewhat like the angels had come for us, "Mr. R-o-s-e-n-thal, Mr. R-o-s-e-n-t-h-a-l!" It was, as you can imagine, a former student.

Thirty-eight years earlier, on our honeymoon, we had been greeted by a student and her parents as we swam in the pool. On one's honeymoon! Good that this girl passed the course!

Former students and their parents have approached me in restaurants, symphonies, and resorts, in several U.S. states, airplanes, Caribbean beaches, and Europe. Can you imagine snorkeling off the coast of Aruba and meeting a former student and his family?

Walking through a square on the outskirts of Nice, France, a former student beckoned me. Celia was visiting her brother, chatting in an outdoor bistro, and yours truly and wife made an entrance. What a great reunion we all had!

One time, I was bothered by what turned out to be a glass splinter in my thumb. After a day of teaching and coaching, I finally went to the emergency room of a local large hospital. Lying on a table being prepared for the surgeon to remove this stubborn glass splinter, the nurse said, "Are you Mr. Rosenthal, my former science teacher?" It's hard for me to recognize many students anyway, let alone when they're wearing a mask, with bright lights glaring, as I was a bit disoriented and lying down! Now that would win the sleuth award of the year for recollection and diagnosis. "Quite happy you gave serious thought to your lessons back then . . . especially since I'm here and now," so I exclaimed. A few chuckles and I was comforted.

It is fascinating, to be sure, watching this new generation enable our country to be the best it can be, and certainly gratifying to know that in my own way I shared (albeit ever so small) a role in this process.

Many of these anecdotes are unique and all are obviously memorable. Although each presented a different challenge and some required an immediate response, all were compelling and made me realize that I was in the middle of the stage, involved with real-life situations. To react appropriately—what an enormous responsibility! Why is it difficult for people to equate this with other professions?

Certainly, my responses to various students have been altered as the years have been added to my résumé. A teacher develops a certain finesse and wisdom in the midst of collaborating with students, parents, and colleagues, and learns "not to sweat the small stuff." The difficult part for me was to learn what was and what was not "small stuff."

The everyday experiences of the teacher are indeed sufficient to warrant volumes of materials. It is, however, my intent to canvas the spectrum of this complex plant, rather than limit the encounters to personal experiences with students and parents.

I am not in any way a presumptuous person; however, *if* this book ever comes to fruition, I could realize a dream of filling a volume of such experiences. It can be demonstrated that in nearly every potentially disruptive situation elucidated above, the common denominator is the absence of a stable home, where parents are available to not only set examples, but to set limits. That guiding philosophy mentioned earlier must be ever present, especially for the adolescent, and these specifics are the testimonials to such tenets.

Wouldn't it be a great innovation to pluck a manual off the shelf that contains step-by-step moves for parents and teachers? That would be a best-seller for sure—equivalent to winning an Oscar or spawning a gold record!

Imagine this scenario: Suppose your son (or daughter) had just received his driver's license and insisted he make his maiden voyage to a friend's home on Halloween night in the midst of a rainstorm. Initially, you hold up this initiation for a moment, procure the manual, and search the table of contents. Driving with license . . . age . . . male/female . . . day/night . . . and on and on, as this text walks one through the minefield of parenting. Well, this is not to be! So for now, wishful thinking is just that . . . wishful!

Result of scenario (one of those real-life situations): You must turn to the final page of this book for the answer. One condition: you must not advance to that site prior to reading the remainder of this book; just a ploy to encourage the reader to keep reading!

It's no secret that when any fan mimics an idol it is meant to be complimentary. I hope the same principle holds true of students as they seek to ridicule their teacher. One wonderful group of writers, editors, journalists, and publishers deemed it necessary to include a drawing of my "disorganized" bookcase in the school newspaper. I admit this wall of books, specimens, and souvenirs was in disarray and, no doubt, required more attention on my part; excuses and rationale were offered, all to no avail.

Suddenly, these students become observant and their attention to detail parallels rocket science. They included an old necktie protruding through a few texts and some petri dishes intentionally left exposed to gather mold spores. They observed various texts "from years gone by" (these students had also become suddenly poetic), included there for certain comparison studies. The drawing included a packaged preserved frog specimen that was a forerunner of that regular jug of specimens and this beat could go on and on.

Their captions amazed me because I had never witnessed such particular attention to and retention of their lessons! I suppose we can now appreciate what can motivate students. Who said they can't do whatever they want to do? The secret lies in aiming at a common target, and this stimulates the adrenalin to achieve an excitement, placing one's teacher up for display. This clever brigade wished to elicit some response from yours truly and they succeeded. I utilized the avenue of "letters to the editor" to plead my case—all in fun, of course.

These youngsters were enjoying themselves at their teacher's expense but I too was satisfied with the attention and the ridicule. This picture is still one of my favorites, tucked away in an album. This story is included here for a touch of "the lighter side." Remember that sense of humor?

Earlier, I mentioned a mountain trip (New Hampshire) activity and another aspect of that trip remains with me. Episodes like these bring out the best *and* the worst in students' behavior patterns. They are especially revealing when youngsters are in an unfamiliar setting and are relied upon to exercise proper judgment.

After nearly three days, 'twas the hour to leave our temporary encampment. Our responsibility was to take all refuse and all remaining foodstuffs with us, a task that required each student to share the load. No sooner had we assisted students with loading their frame backpacks than Tina announced she had sprained her ankle and was unable to carry her backpack! We hastily mobilized our troopers to pick up the slack by dividing Tina's pack. Soon messages filtered through the groups that Tina's sprained ankle was equivalent to a "sprained eyelash." It seemed that this young woman could think of no one but herself. She had shifted her load to others and caused us much unnecessary concern for her welfare!

As we descended the heights, I detected the merit in the messages that previously had filtered down to me. Later, when questioned, Tina denied all accusations and continued to falsify her feelings. Realizing no admittance for such behavior would be forthcoming, I decided to spell out to Tina the dangers, the poor judgment, the mistrust, and dishonesty perpetrated on her peers and her teachers. This young woman required a lesson on integrity. I have always maintained that part of my responsibility as a teacher was to try to instill a certain amount of probity or honesty into their psyche.

I certainly never expected any sort of perfection, yet as I continued to work with such students, I expected to see gradual changes to some sound, moral, sincere principles. This is the sort of accomplishment I found exhilarating and uplifting, much more so than filling in a space with the letter A or B!

Again and again, I expected these students to leave me at year's end with a sense of personal accomplishment, some small personal growth with honor first and foremost in addition to their academic achievements. Some say this is "too much to expect at this age"; I say never too much to expect if teachers truly wish to make a difference in the lives of their students.

To jest with youngsters, especially adolescents, can totally backfire. These boys and girls will forever present a mixed bag of emotions; I learned this with difficulty and rather quickly. Their sense of humor, or total lack thereof, can be devastating for them and their teachers. The following is a brief example to demonstrate how an intended innocent humorous remark "backfired."

Students walk and run around with untied sneakers; it's a style, they say (?). After watching this for a few years, I believed they were . . . simply too excited about school? No. Possibly in too much haste to arrive to class on time? I think not. Maybe just plain lazy? Take your pick! A thought: These students would have made great dancers because they had so much practice skipping over and around those dangling laces without missing a skip (beat)!

Soon I noticed some students with one lace tied and the other untied. Could this be a new fad? Similar to wearing one earring? These incidents became so prevalent they prompted me to respond in a rather nonchalant manner. Specifically, I zeroed in on Charlie, for no particular reason, only to include him in my humor. Left sneaker lace tied neatly each day while the right sneaker lace wiggled like a snake on the ground and waved like a flag in the wind.

"Good job with that left lace, Charlie! Keep practicing with that right one and you'll catch on!" Wow, like the proverbial ton of bricks!" "Mr. R., I have a big problem with that right one; something is wrong with my coordination and fine motor skills on that side!" Immediately came my apology, no questions asked at the time, and our line of communication remained intact. Later, the guidance staff briefed me on this "ailment." I was compelled to either satisfy my curiosity or remove this sort of humor (?) from my repertoire; I did both. This seemingly trivial situation might explain that fine line between silly and serious in the middle school. This may also explain the expression "walking a tight rope." It certainly explains a lot about teaching school.

I heard from Philomena's mother in response to my advertisement for math tutoring. With all these scenarios, I'm sure it's obvious that the teacher doesn't "only" present the lesson and leave until the next session—that would be fairly easy. In my experience, there were "always" contingencies, ramifications, and inevitably convoluted situations. These conditions play a role in the student-teacher relationship, some of what teaching is all about.

When I first met Philomena, she was living temporarily (as it turned out) with her mother, her sister, and mother's second husband. Some time earlier, Philomena had lived and subsequently left her father and his second wife, who were living in New Mexico. (I believe one now is either lost in this saga or it sounds familiar and is deciphered easily!)

Apparently, Philomena thought living with her mother would pose fewer restrictions on her and her living habits. She had been expelled from school in New Mexico and was now enrolled in the local school system; however, she sure miscalculated her mother's intentions for her to attend classes regularly, study, have ample time for other school-based activities and part-time employment, and be home at reasonable hours. These were not extraordinary demands, just routine and pleasurable for most young adults—but not for Philomena!

I came on the scene and for several weeks Phil (for short) responded most admirably. Her math grade went from F to C and then to B. Other subjects (that I was also to work on) followed suit and Phil seemed to be on the proper track.

Soon Phil became quite antagonistic toward her stepfather and her younger sister. House rules were abandoned, homework became unimportant, and she met "friends" at her part-time job who hindered her academic progress—definitely unhealthy company. As I detected this change of heart, I made my feelings known to Phil. "We cannot and will not continue our working together if there is no cooperation on your part." I began to see myself going in circles while wasting much time and her mother's money, but I continued to struggle to maintain some decorum with our lessons as our own relationship was waning.

Within days, I received a telephone call from New Mexico; Phil thanked me for trying to help her and she stated she wished to try living with her father and his "new" family once again. About a month later, Phil's mother called me to prepare a plan for Phil, who returned to study for a GED (General Education Degree) exam. Phil canceled the next two scheduled tutoring sessions and the last communication I received from her mother was "Phil was incarcerated in New Mexico."

What began as mild-mannered, straightforward tutoring sessions changed to a journey laden with strife, struggles, obstacles, and all sorts of other serious problems. Again and again, I had refused to give up on this young woman. I watched a smart, talented, sensitive, articulate youngster accomplish much with very few odds in her favor. She seemed to have her life under control and her work was challenging and engaging for her.

However, I could not take the place of stability in her home. I could not prevail as the influence on her that I wished to be. I also thought we came close to sustaining a trusting, loving relationship. In the end, I may have thought wrong, yet it was important for me to have tried and to have had the opportunity to influence, in spite of the outcome.

Billy, a student with a similar background and family history but miles apart when it came to disposition and attitude, was undergoing therapy to enable him to control his vehement temper. This youngster arrived at school angry, carried this attitude with(in) him throughout the day, and left school in the same condition as he arrived.

Billy was the focus of many a meeting as all of his teachers and other specialists convened to assemble a plan we could all live with. Rules of behavior for him were the number one priority, with limited restrictions and various concessions put into place. We were also concerned with his meager academic progress, a problem that exacerbated his already low self-esteem. One problem fed off another and this cycle was in full gear.

One day, Billy's anger and disappointment over not being selected as a player on the tennis team prompted him to kick in the car door of my colleague—an action that was meant for my automobile! Similar autos, similar year and color. Eventually, Billy admitted he was responsible. He paid for the damage, apologized, and promised he would not resort to such actions in the future.

Increased professional therapy for him and increased efforts to hold him accountable to contracts were devised by the staff. Now that all of the above were put into place, and we were all privy to the problems *and* plans, we believed we could succeed. And we did succeed in making a difference in Billy's life.

Another student, Ian, possessed a rather loveable disposition. When I first met him, he offered to assist me with preparing the experimental apparatus, a time-consuming task. By now, the reader is aware that I was willing to accept assistance, especially since the "price was right." During subsequent weeks, Ian's calamitous exam scores were not indicative of his ability, and I wondered if I was contributing to his academic demise. He was involved with other extracurricular activities, yet his grades continued to plummet. There existed a reticence on his part to ease up on time devoted to nonacademic endeavors and concentrate more on his studies. Ian sort of reminded me of so many other students who will do anything, even house chores, to forestall hitting the books.

On many an occasion, Ian was made aware of this lack of prioritizing his responsibilities. The more messages he received along these lines, the more antagonistic he became. For a boy who began the school year with a pleasant attitude that carried through for several months to arrive at a complete turnabout was disappointing. "All" Ian did was put me to a test: how long, how far, would I allow him to go it his own way! His antagonism came to an abrupt halt when I made him an offer I did not think he would refuse. This is where his positive attitude took hold.

I would allow Ian to continue to assist me provided I saw improvement with his studies. The ultimate "award": he could be the beneficiary of a summer month of pure joy for him. I invited him to be my laboratory assistant as I taught a summer enrichment course on Comparative Anatomy. This time the price was right, from his standpoint! He was an asset to my course and demonstrated his ability to follow instructions and make responsible decisions. The fact that I depended upon him while I taught sent an important message to him, a message that also made a difference in his life.

One of my most rewarding, inspiring, productive, and memorable summers was devoted to teaching a biology class to African American women. This was an experience I will always remember and cherish. Some of these women migrated to Boston from the South, some grew up in Boston, and a few crossed a sea and arrived here while still in their early twenties.

Each lady had her own story to tell. They communicated with me about their early struggles and how hard they worked to maintain stability within their homes. The stories of their sacrifices mimicked what we read about in our history books. Their trials and tribulations alone could be the subject of a thesis, one that exemplified ingenuity, courage, and devotion to family and work.

Later in life, these women took advantage of the opportunities afforded them and demonstrated how labor, patience, and perseverance (the Rosenthal motto) can allow one to attain a goal. Each lady, ranging in age from about thirty-five to fifty-five years old (Remember, no one dares ask a lady her age!), owned and operated a business.

Their businesses covered the gamut from local food market, nail shop, beauty salon, dress shop, and laundromat to sports shop and fish market. These entrepreneurs possessed a few major incentives in common, motivation being at the top of their list.

To observe these women in class and have the opportunity to witness their study habits was indeed refreshing. They were relentless in pursuing their goals, hence challenging me from day one, and were another classic example of working, studying, and learning together.

Their ultimate goal was the honor of becoming a registered nurse; the final course required of them was my biology class, prior to entering Northeastern University's nursing program. At the time, they were enrolled in the ODWIN (Opening Doors Wider in Nursing) program in Roxbury, Massachusetts.

The course was difficult, for I was required to present much material in a brief amount of time. This condition added to an already complex course, but these women met every challenge confronting them. Their days and evenings were extremely well organized as they combined studies with business and family matters.

A few of these students had daughters who were enrolled in Northeastern University's nursing program and I invited the young ladies to join their mothers for our laboratory sessions. What a poignant sight to watch a daughter assisting her mother with the lesson. Need I elaborate that I learned much? These students graduated with honors.

Their's was a "gift" I gladly accepted, a memento that to this day is displayed in my home office. An 8"x11" picture frame with some hand-drawn animal pictures and a drawing of a door with the words: "Thanks from your summer biology students, ODWIN, Inc."

In another summer biology session, I realized what an uphill battle I had with the ten students before me. All of these students had at least two concerns in common: they had dropped out of school, were trying (?) to make a comeback, and they all came from unstable, dysfunctional homes. How does a teacher begin to motivate and encourage such teenagers in such a brief time span?

Teaching summer school was never easy. I believe this teaching puts more demands on the teacher and student. Students are exposed to a lot of material in a matter of weeks. Not much time for the teacher to dwell on one aspect, not much time to elaborate on any one phase of the course, and not much time to establish and nurture a meaningful relationship—all of which are necessary elements in teaching.

The responsibility was mind-boggling and always forced me to re-vamp my course requirements while maintaining the integrity of the course. My approach was intense, and rules and expectations were spelled out to the letter, as were the consequences. My speech continued: "Work hard every day, do your homework every day, and attend class every day. I'm here to help every day, and if you keep this in mind, you will succeed."

It seemed routine, but certainly not for these teenagers. They were accustomed to making their own rules and altering them to suit themselves. They had few, if any, role models and acted on impulse. I could never ease up on the work and I pleaded with them to show up, since they were well aware that three absences were cause for dismissal.

As the summer sessions ended, we celebrated with a 70 percent "survival" rate. For me, the results were a bit disappointing because the three students who did have the opportunity to celebrate had eliminated themselves simply on the basis of attendance.

This was another situation where smart students craved discipline and went astray. My hands were tied when such specific rules were broken. I could always justify my grades; however, there was never any compromise when attendance was at stake. "If you fail to attend class, you obviously miss the lesson; if you miss the lesson, you set yourself up for failure."

A brief scenario regarding another summer session in another city where a student pleaded with the director for admission to my tenth grade algebra class: This girl was often truant, involved with drugs, on probation, and on the verge of being expelled from school. She talked her way into admittance nearly a week late to my class. I witnessed her excuses as we (Cindy, her stepfather, the director, and I) conceded that she be given this last chance. Her initial class was spent copying her neighbor's homework. The following day, Cindy passed in "her" homework with the original author's name erased and her name substituted. Now I knew why Ray told me he could not find his homework assignment that he assured me he had completed.

Can one imagine this girl resorting to such tactics after so much time and energy had been exhausted on her behalf! Heartbreaking as it was, I requested Cindy be dropped from the course. I also suggested other alternatives be instituted for this young woman. In other words, a quick fix (in this instance) was not the route to take.

I cannot blame the educators for trying. Problems arise and the first inclination is often: "Go to summer school." Come September, all work is made up and the student is ready to resume a regular full-time program. One can understand that the above statement is indeed an oversimplification; it does not necessarily work out with that happy ending!

This final entry is by far not the least, and demonstrates that "Oh, have the times changed!"

A rare and unexpected turn of events ensued during my third or fourth year of teaching. One of my former students suggested that I call her sister for a date! In no way had I ever as much as hinted for such a suggestion. Remember what I said about how honest these youngsters are, with (usually) no hidden agendas and no inhibitions? Students say what is on their minds, especially after asking all sorts of personal questions. Oh, have the times changed!

I suppose I reminded them of an older brother who happened to be their teacher, more so than this now older adult. Weeks elapsed and I finally agreed to meet this young lady for a bowling date. Ultimately, my date's girlfriend and escort joined us and we became a double date. To confine this scenario to brevity and avoid additional embarrassment, my date's girlfriend became my wife about two years later. This is one student whom I wish to thank; however, no contact could be accomplished.

Do you suppose my student lost patience during my extended courtship (considering, after all, that adolescent courtship is of the "brevity" variety!) and abandoned any thought that such a relationship would ensue or endure? At least it was fortunate that a former student had initiated this introduction. I could never have accepted such an offer otherwise!

No intention to present this scenario as a "dangling carrot" or any such enticement to "join the ranks." Nor do I, in any way, intimate that this profession will provide a conduit for matrimonial bliss! It's included here to illustrate another aspect of the human side of the teacher and students. These everyday encounters exemplify "the genuine school life"—the school, the life, as they blend.

15

THE ADMINISTRATION

School administrators have much responsibility, more so than most people realize. Since I have worked with several administrators, I believe I am qualified to state that these educators enjoy (or should I write "entertain"?) difficult "living quarters"! There exists so much complexity that there is now, in many schools, a distinction between the assistant principal and the assistant to the principal (often the newly created position), both positions being necessary.

If I were to describe the principal, I'd say that this is the person who stops the buck-passing, the person who is in charge, the person who tries to encourage the innovator and has patience with the rebellious and the talented. To be sure, this environment has its share of the nonconformist (teachers and students), yet as the past president of DuPont said, it's "the uncommon man/woman" who makes an organization grow (referring to other organizations). The principal must not only communicate with the angels, he or she must talk with the superintendent, colleagues from other schools in and out of the system, custodial staff, teachers, parents/guardians, PTA reps, and still keep abreast of the current educational process. For now, I will not mention the life span of a principal! Again, I remember the phrase that was highlighted in my mind as I attended several seminars—tolerance for the ambiguity—the bottom line, as far as I'm concerned.

The principal must see not only the black-and-white sides of issues but must be aware of the ever-present gray spectrum. There are rules for just about any aspect of human behavior, but are we to allow ourselves to be consumed by them and not question their validity, or are these rules ambiguous?

The principal must consider *why* the rules (of conduct) were fragmented, *why* a student is acting out, or *why* a student threatened and intimidated a classmate or swore at a teacher. Imagine all sorts of sets of extenuating circumstances! There will always be rules to follow, there will always be limits, and there will always be consequences. When students are guided in understanding this premise, they are indeed better equipped to live their lives.

Mistakes will be made by all parties (adolescents and, yes, adults, too) and problems will arise. We must admit our errors, learn from them, acknowledge the ambiguities that inevitably come into play, and go forward with an even greater determination to succeed; this is the productive approach.

Dr. Lewis Thomas, in his *The Lives of a Cell*, states that "ambiguity seems to be an essential, indispensable element for the transfer of information . . . by words, where matters of real importance are concerned. If it were not for the capacity for ambiguity . . . we would have no way of recognizing the layers of counterpoint in meaning." We don't have to be locked into the situation at hand, we have license to divert, and therein lies the secret, the code, and the magic and wonder of being human, and being able to make ingenious connections from past to present!

Many additional responsibilities are lauded on the superhuman principal, who seems to be denied such "feeling of routine." Forget what their desk resembles; just recognizing the principal from behind stacks of literature is in itself challenging. At one time, I had the opportunity to shadow the principal and I was the one who felt like performing the "disappearing act."

The principal often arrived at school or for a meeting long before most teachers were awake. He may have already attended a parent conference, only to be interrupted by telephone calls and incidents requiring incessant note taking. There may have been a brief urgent message to be dictated or spoken over the intercom, or sent via the computer.

Next, he might have been off to observe a few special classes in session, all before 8:00 A.M.

I found it very interesting to be present and observe the atmosphere during interviews for prospective teachers in the public schools and student candidates for the private arena. One such interview in a private school in particular remained a poignant memory for me. I didn't always agree with the "principal's principles," but it was refreshing to be invited to express my opinion on certain issues.

Enter Joseph and his mother; he was applying to enter the school's fall session. During the course of the interview, it was apparent that this candidate met all the necessary requirements (and then some) to be admitted to the freshman class. I believed this student would benefit from such an education and would be an asset to the school. Joseph's mother then asked, somewhat dubiously, if it was mandatory for her son to attend "chapel services." It was obvious that she was concerned about religious overtones. She received an affirmative answer; later, this resulted in a not-so-favorable admittance decision for Joseph.

I questioned the headmaster about his ruling. His response was definitive, but I detected a slight defensive posture. He revealed to me that because the family had asked for this concession (i.e., to be excused from chapel), they would ask for other concessions! I thought twice before I calmly and firmly asked the headmaster why he didn't explain to Joseph's mother that chapel service only entailed listening to routine pep talks, but with no religious connotations.

This entire communication and outcome is now history, but it was disheartening, disappointing, and disgraceful for me at the time. I was not convinced that justice prevailed!

Years later, I did have several opportunities to witness more tolerant and democratic interviews, a fact that restored my faith in the selection process. It was gratifying to talk with prospective teachers and veteran teachers whose only wish was to make a difference in the lives of middle school and high school students. They were goal orientated and continued to work and study long hours to realize their goals.

Whenever I interviewed a candidate for a teaching position, I did my best to establish a rather informal setting, thereby putting this teacher at ease. There was never any hint of pretension, deception, or suppression, simply a calm, smooth, honest discussion. This was a natural approach for me since I am by nature an informal person.

All principals are content when students learn. All principals delight in the fact that learning can and does take place in a safe environment. I now allude to safety because that is probably the number one concern (and responsibility) of all principals. Without this, no learning can take place. When students feel they are in safe environs, they can accomplish just about anything they wish.

Many (if not most) schools now have a safety plan in place that addresses quite a variety of possible emergency situations. Many schools prefer not to create an armed-camp type of atmosphere. What a horrible way to attend schools with security officers on patrol. There does exist, however, a federally sponsored program of "cops in the schools," undertaken fairly successfully in some cities. The officer is a school resource person who is involved in some teaching and counseling, and a relationship is developed between the students and the law enforcement community.

This concern for safety in the schools is analogous to the air-raid drills we conducted in the '50s and '60s. I remember designated areas were made available for such emergencies. Some families actually had bomb shelters built in their back yards, and these shelters were stocked with all sorts of emergency goods. Safety concerns such as these are real, they are existent, they are factual, and they are undeniable.

Every decade brings with it different challenges and the teachers will, and do, approach these concerns with the dedication and commitment necessary to make what I call "midcourse corrections"; it is expected of the teacher!

Because I am alluding primarily to the teachers, I intend to emphasize the principal's role as it involves, to some extent, the teacher. A sure-fire method for the principal to become aware of the curriculum is to observe the teachers and students in action. As the school comes alive with all sorts of movement and rhetoric, the principal can grasp a feeling about the effectiveness of the teacher. By witnessing these most important interactions between students and staff, the principal may offer suggestions that are intended to refine various teaching techniques. The professional who deems these evaluations as constructive will learn much and be better prepared to offer the most effective instruction in and out of the classroom. Remember, much of the learning for student *and* teacher is an ongoing process throughout the entire plant.

While on this evaluation subject, I am compelled to add that I believe whoever evaluates another person must be sensitive, patient, intelligent, compassionate, sincere, and committed. This person has an enormous responsibility. This evaluation process is indeed both time consuming and rewarding for all parties concerned and an invaluable tool for the preparation of the teacher.

Prospective teachers should read some materials about the performance standards as set forth by various school systems based on the Education Reform Act of 1993. Many school districts and teacher associations agree on performance standards. Although it's easy to be intimidated by the numerous rules and regulations, prospective teachers simply need an overview of the expectations.

Some of the general topics an evaluation might include are instructional competence (planning and preparation, learning environment, methodology, subject matter, and respect for human differences) and professional characteristics (quality of relationships, professional growth, and managerial responsibilities).

One principal with whom I worked had a genuine awareness of curriculum and of teachers in action, and I used his availability in our annual mountain trip, which involved managing groups of students studying flora, fauna, and rock and mineral formations in New Hampshire.

Groups of students were selected on the basis of gender, compatibility, and temperament, and because I had some influence in the formation of the groups, I decided that Jared would be assigned to a group of students led by the principal. Jared was the student who demanded much attention throughout the year. He was smart, alert, and well liked by his peers, yet put every teacher to the test. Whenever there appeared to be an opportunity to deviate from the rules, Jared would be leading the line. This young man not only bent and broke the rules, he aimed for complete annihilation. And, naturally, in his path were victims and evidence of his destructive ways. He resembled a human hurricane when aroused and we all tried our best to prepare for his outbursts prior to their actual touchdown!

I had ambivalent feeling about allowing Jared to join us on such a trip of three days and two nights. Aware that our principal was assisting, I decided to test this principal's fortitude. For several months, I had lived with Jared and attempted every teaching technique known to humankind to harness his energy, attitude, and temperament. I believed our principal's turn to witness his behavior firsthand had at long last arrived. This man was now in command, in charge, and was given full responsibility of Jared and his group. As several groups hiked through the mountain trails, my auditory nerve detected familiar commands directed toward Jared. For sure, sound does travel about 1,100 feet per second in air.

I believe an administrator should *truly* have similar experiences as her staff and, of course, not lose that touch with the students. Even though I sort of expected it of this principal, I received a "thank you!" from him when we came down from the mountain. I do not advise this sort of technique for the beginners; however, this is another example of how a teacher's disposition is shaped during the course of a career. Beginners, beware lest you remain beginners!

The principal's school day may come to a close but the evening will soon begin with several communications, written and oral, as this person sorts out all the ramifications. The budget will also need some quiet evening attention, a school committee meeting or PTA meeting might beckon, or a school function may be on the docket. In other words, this "twenty-five-hour-a-day" commitment can be taxing to the system (human, that is)!

The assistant principal is another superhuman who has the right to wear the infamous Superman or Superwoman outfit. Can you believe that this educator, who also has an advanced degree or two, and may teach a class, will invariably have the distinction (with honor) to take charge of the cafeteria? This is mentioned because it takes talent and a whistle to take charge. This is where the troops enter the scene; teachers are a necessity to help monitor this environment. This assistance will be built into the teachers' schedules, with other assignments that may or may not require advanced degrees. The staff members arrive at this "activity" with much trepidation for there never exists any definite lesson plan.

Not only will the assistant principal help with staff evaluations but he will play a major role in handling much of the discipline in the school. Discipline could be the title of a book in itself; at this time, I merely want to point out that the teacher will be able to avail herself of this all-important resource.

Order in the classroom and throughout the school is necessary for any learning to be accomplished, yet many teachers are totally unprepared to handle the undisciplined student. Oft times the "learn as you go" syndrome takes effect and this can be most uncomfortable for the teacher because there are an infinite number of variables to consider when exercising one's disciplinary tactics. This is another important weapon in the teacher's arsenal that must be learned to become effective when working (not only teaching) with students.

When an effective school-home relationship develops, the problems with discipline diminish. This relationship entails trust, patience, time, and loads of empathy. It takes nurturing to spawn meaningful dialogues that eventually lead to positive actions.

This school-home relationship is another important aspect in the life of the teacher; in fact, it should be a major priority. The teacher's willingness to foster a healthy relationship will put this teacher in good stead. There are no guarantees that life will be easy, but I do believe life with the adolescent will become easier.

In the 1997–1998 school year, 3.2 million suspensions and 90,000 expulsions were given to some of the 46 million public school students in the United States. What a disgrace! These figures (from Chris Chapman of the National Center for Educational Statistics) reveal the seriousness of the discipline problem.

The assistant to the principal (a luxury not available in most schools) extends the (school) life of the principal. This person assists the principal with clerical details in addition to attending many an in-school meeting involving special students' needs and specific programs that must be adhered to. Again, there are legal aspects that must be recognized in dealing with various special educational programs, and the needs of these students are brought to the attention of the teachers often through this liaison.

New teachers learn how to communicate with so many "specialists" in addition to other peers, parents and guardians, and, of course, students—so much so, that at times he will wonder why he did not major in communications!

16

THE PAPER TRAIL

For me, paperwork is like a railroad track made up of endless strands of paper, heading off into infinity.

There are grades for just about all sorts of activities, and whether we like it or not, grading as the method of evaluating students is here to stay. Obviously, several methods can be utilized to evaluate students; however, the grade (letter or number) route seems to be the most popular. For me, grading students was a difficult and tedious task because I combined my objectivity with my subjectivity. I tried to think of the growth and improvement exhibited in all aspects of the course, thereby demonstrating to my students that my grades were based on a multifaceted approach—that is, I took their genuine effort into consideration.

There are grades for all sorts of oral and written reports, class work, homework, effort, notebooks, projects, and the inevitable exams, oral and written. Put all this in perspective three or four times per year as a summation and there is a resulting myriad of paperwork that involves much time, effort, sensitivity, and accuracy to accomplish. Who was it who said the teacher's work ends about 3:00 P.M.! Surely, the computer is a super assistance nowadays, but we must keep in mind that although this machine might compute the grade, it certainly does not "arrange"

(compile) the grade! No question that technology is a savior when referring to a vast number of chores. We must now keep in mind that
there comes a price with this technology. Other problems arise with its
use; it cannot think *and* it does not always follow orders. The paper trail
is diminished but the vigilance must continue.

There is the ever-present existence of reports and memos that must be
prepared for proper and timely communications. Student progress reports are indeed necessary to communicate with the home scene because
this is a vital segment of the evaluation process written about earlier.

And don't forget the reports to other departments, interschool and
intraschool. Again, these reports are essential to keep abreast of current
events, including interdisciplinary activities and examining the possibility of incorporating the same into one's own curriculum.

As stated earlier, the computer indeed is of great benefit, but it is not
to be construed as an "in place of" tool! Jotting down a memorandum at
the appropriate time can save loads of grief at a later date. On several
occasions, I would pull out many such notes from my briefcase just like
one would pull out tickets from a hat. Next, I would arrange these notes
in some sort of meaningful (to me) manner and then proceed to act
upon them (or at least some of them). We can say "thank God" for
e-mail, provided one has easy access to a computer or walks about with
a laptop. Can you picture a teacher walking around a school with a laptop? (A *few* do!) No teacher on this planet would ever have the luxury
of having both hands and mind free to manipulate this unless they were
in a self-induced solitary confinement mode. Just want to interject (because I mentioned that word *e-mail*): There may be a need to monitor
the students' use of the Internet and the e-mail. Parents may have to
help regulate what is acceptable as the turf is being surfed, considering
there are about 335 million e-mail addresses and that number is constantly growing. The need to monitor is a reality.

Most of these varied approaches are fodder for a teacher's evaluation
of a student and also for an assessment of the curriculum. Once again,
it is important for the teacher to resign herself to the fact that the above
responsibilities will consume much more time than the time "spent"
teaching in the classroom! That's *Reality 101: What it's really like to be
a teacher . . . and teach, too!*

17

SPECIAL EVENTS

Attendance at many special events is voluntary, although some events do require a physical presence. Monetary rewards for overtime, time and a half, or double time are nonexistent, yet what a pleasurable way to witness students outside the confines of the classroom. For me, attending these events was enlightening, stimulating, exciting, and necessary.

Open house (back-to-school night) is, in most instances, the first contact a parent or guardian has with the school. This is usually an evening event where teachers have the opportunity to introduce their courses. Remember the saying about first impressions? Well, this is it! This evening is rather special for all parties to introduce themselves and place faces with names (or is it names with faces?).

This coming together is not to discuss individual situations, but is a great opportunity for the teacher to not only outline the course but to explain the more pertinent expectations involved in the discipline—that is, homework assignments, notebooks, textbooks, and reasonable decorum in the classroom. There might even be more general questions entertained from the parents and guardians. Of course, it is expected that the teacher naturally put his best foot forward. This also includes an enhanced physical environment. Whatever subject is being taught, I always felt that the classroom decor should be an obvious indicator of the subject matter. Time and energy on the part of students and teachers should be devoted to living in a room that is alive with the most pertinent subject-matter information available. Attention to all of these details will make for a successful beginning to a long, productive school year.

Parent-teacher conferences are designed specifically to discuss individual student progress or the lack thereof. This is the time and place where teacher and parent must communicate their concerns and, if need be, plan a course of action. This is the time when all sorts of interests are "put on the table," and significant issues resolved. At times, all parties will agree to have the student attend such meetings. Several techniques can be employed; however, all are intended to put parent, teacher, and student on the same wavelength.

These meetings are often scheduled during a team-meeting block. These blocks are periods of time built into the teachers' program where a specific group (team) of teachers' schedules coincide, thereby enabling all concerned to attend. Of course, there are occasions when the principal, his assistants, or guidance personnel will be present. Teachers come to realize that teaching is often a team approach. Many times I would espouse my philosophy that "We [the entire staff] are all on the same team."

Parent-teacher association meetings are another vehicle for communication with the community. This is another excellent opportunity for parents and teachers to work together for a common good. Many topics are discussed, including the proverbial "bake sale." (Please do not think I'm making light of this, but I would like to point out that there do exist other projects!) This association also sponsors several cultural events for students throughout the year and is constantly searching for additional activities to enhance the school program.

A teacher representative is almost always present at these meetings, although attendance for other teachers is voluntary. It's good to keep in mind that it never hurts to meet the people who devote their time and energy to the cause of education.

Special events come to mind when I think of the all-school events, namely the nearly professional (I call them) productions. I have attended plays such as *Mame, Carousel, Annie Get Your Gun, Music Man,* and *Fiddler on the Roof,* to name a few. I swelled with pride, as though these youngsters were members of my family; I suppose I could say the players were an extension of my family. It was always a treat to watch my students on stage, playing a role, giving their all, and being proud of their accomplishments.

Some of these same students, just hours prior to their on-stage appearance, gave me excuses for incomplete assignments and the like. I, of course, always backed off on my homework assignments and deferred to the music director during these star-studded programs. I cannot play good guy because this "back-off policy" was school initiated. Obviously, this teacher purchased a ticket (full price) and sat wherever he could; in other words, there was no special treatment for dear teacher. Just in case some reader entertains the thought—no, there never existed any so-called bribery!

The drama productions mirrored many musical performances during the year. Concerts proved to parents and friends that their money was well spent for those music lessons. I, on occasion, would listen to a rehearsal. At times, the piece being played was unrecognizable to any human auditory nerve, but when the curtain was raised, the tones and sounds were the food of love, and these kids were beckoned to play on.

I always marveled at how the music department could contemporaneously arrange such extravaganzas; this was a testimonial to their talents as teachers. Many music students were beginners, some had very little savvy, and others had extensive training with vocal and or instrumental lessons. How the music teacher puts this conglomeration of talent together is mind-boggling to me!

Sports "plays" an enormous part of any school program, often coming under the aegis of an athletic program. Fall sports, winter sports, and spring sports were all part of the athletic program usually overseen by the physical education teacher. Because this one teacher cannot possibly manage or coach all teams and teach regularly scheduled classes, teachers within (sometimes outside) the school agree to assume the compensated responsibility of coaching a team. This is without a doubt an enormous responsibility, from checking on physical exams initially to the ultimate final awards presentations. There is a vast array of experiences involved in this area. Several meetings and practices with players, the various permission slips, notification of other school personnel for reasons such as academic and citizenship standing (i.e., eligibility) to equipment and budgetary concerns—all are time consuming but well worth the effort.

Sports activities involve a different sort of communication, a kind of informal "coming together" that breeds confidence in players. The trust and commitment that ensues between the team and the coach is invaluable and this is where many a student is "turned on." "Turned on and tuned in" are the passwords that have enabled students to communicate their feelings, thereby enabling them to be proud of their accomplishments. It is the dream of the teacher that through the sport (acting as a confidence builder) the students will transmit a vibrant outlook to their studies and other school-related programs.

The teacher may never have previously played or coached the sport he or she is intending to coach, but that is not become the primary prerequisite for the job. The teacher need only have some insight and understanding of how to "live" with young adults, and the ability to allow each team member to be given the opportunity to exercise her talents to the fullest. If the team won, then that is a bonus; if the team lost (a dominant trait in my coaching experience), then the teacher needed to accentuate the positive aspects of the game. I always encouraged my team; we expected to win against whomever we played, regardless of the odds against us. The tenacity of my team made us successful on and off the tennis court!

There will arise many problems and obstacles working with adolescents, yet if the teacher, this special adult in their life, is willing to devote his life to teaching—to preparing, to nurturing, to encouraging, to having patience, understanding, and tolerance—then this teacher will certainly become a teacher . . . and teach, too!

18

CLASSES AND THE CURRICULUM

This may be the last chapter in this saga but certainly not the least; in fact, this could be the first chapter.

The classroom is where the action is, the firing line, or in other words, where all the stops are pulled to ensure safety and provide an environment that is mutually conducive to teaching and learning.

Because different disciplines warrant different classroom organization, the teacher determines which setting is best for a particular class. To some, this physical organization of the furniture might not be significant; however, this set-up can be tantamount to presenting a well-planned lesson and can contribute much to the success of the lesson. Minor as it might seem initially, this is an important detail that the teacher must consider when planning many an activity.

A "lecture" might necessitate chairs and desks set up in rows, whereas a circular arrangement might be in order when discussions ensue. Less formal situations, such as laboratory (science, music, arts, crafts, physical education, etc.) classes, will obviously foster more movement around the classroom and may require a different arrangement.

Several years ago, I shared a classroom with a teacher who insisted that his classes be organized in an oblate spheroid manner. My particular classes could not handle this arrangement and we therefore encountered a major problem that was solved by compromise. When he taught (in the mornings), he enjoyed his roundabout atmosphere and re-arranged the setting for my afternoon classes. Before I left the room in the afternoons, I rearranged the seats to his satisfaction. Can one possibly imagine putting such a situation into one's teaching plans? Remember what I wrote earlier regarding the word "tolerance"? This was the epitome of tolerance—for my peer.

Because I alluded to space and overcrowding in chapter 1, I now return briefly to this important scenario.

According to the U.S. Department of Education (2000), more than 20 percent of U.S. schools have more students than they were built to serve. Overcrowded schools report being more likely than other schools to have problems with building space, features, and climate control.

Therefore, it becomes increasingly evident that the wear-and-tear that rising enrollments put on schools is taking its toll on education, and teachers may have to contend with such inadequacies. If teachers are more fortunate, they can be thankful; however, nothing—not even the space for the classroom itself—should be taken for granted.

I always considered my classroom as my home away from home. I will not admit to sleeping in this environment, but I will admit to undertaking nearly every other human endeavor in this environment. I would sit at my desk surrounded by several student contributions, whether suspended from a ceiling panel, plastered to a wall, or secured to a desk or counter. All were signs of accomplishment, dedication, interest, and commitment; this environment was as much theirs as mine.

To ponder the messages and communications conveyed in this room is mind-boggling to me. To think that so many interactions can begin here and play such a significant role in the lives of the people who occupy the seats is amazing, and a fact I never took for granted.

The classroom is where all the action takes place, the place where students are hopefully comfortable; where they can make mistakes and learn from them, where students can take chances, and hopefully the place that will conjure up pleasant memories and even a spot of nostalgia when they begin to reminisce (and show their age)!

This is also the place where the teacher is on stage, performing like an actor, often without a script, receiving vibrations from an audience—an audience with mixed emotions and not all on the same page as the conductor. Could it be possible that learning is happening while there exists the proverbial "different strokes coming from different folks"?

Before I continue with the more mundane, I must not forget that the teacher also has the responsibility to make sure the lighting, temperature, and ventilation of this chamber are functioning properly; these are often overlooked by teachers yet important for obvious reasons. Again, this activity might have to be inserted into the teacher's lesson plan if not on the "to-do" notes. Details, details, and more details—all become an important part of the instructor's life; the better this teacher becomes at addressing these details, the more effective she is. This is where we all hear the word *organization*, because a teacher without organization is not an effective teacher!

The personality and character of the teacher are revealed by the physical setting of his classroom. Different teachers add a personal touch to their surroundings, whether collections of materials from their own experiences (travels, etc.) or drawings, pictures, artifacts, or specimens; all add a special flavor to the interior decorating. After all, if this is the place where many people will live and work for thirty or more weeks, shouldn't the atmosphere reflect the personality of the people working there?

As our school experiences change, our curriculum must keep pace like the pacemaker paces the beat of the heart. Teachers' content materials are mercurial by nature and these materials must be relevant and incessantly updated. Regardless of the discipline, teachers are unquestionably revamping the ever-changing curriculum. God is probably the only one who could help the teacher who entertains any thought of incorporating the same lessons into his or her teaching plans year after year.

Much of the excitement in teaching comes from the new faces each year, and along with this are the new thoughts and ideas being communicated. In fact, another huge plus to the profession is (I believe) the "new" beginning each year.

Robert and Michele Root-Bernstein write about synthesizing education. They believe, like many others in "implementing a multi-disciplinary approach—placing arts on an equal footing with the sciences, and integrating the curriculum by using common descriptive language."

"Education must focus on the trunk of the tree of knowledge revealing the ways in which branches, twigs, and leaves all merge." Their bottom line is "The point of education is to create whole people who can focus the accumulated wisdom of human experience into illuminated patches of splendor."

To use our means toward this end makes teaching a most admirable, rewarding profession. The circumstances where teacher and student can work together and thrive is, by all means, a success story.

A good technique to enhance a class lesson is always the guest speaker route. These guests truly allow the lessons to take on a relevancy, and grant students a contact with "real" people. The organization of such activities is quite time consuming, however; if the teachers' homework is completed with efficiency, the innovations can make for unforgettable classroom experiences! A few of these experiences will corroborate what was written earlier regarding patience, a sense of humor, understanding, composure, self-control, and humility.

I had recently moved my classes into a newly renovated laboratory and our guest physicist was explaining momentum, forces, and the laws of motion. He was trying to emphasize his point and suddenly, to my surprise, pulled a hammer from his bag of tricks and smacked the countertop, shattering the entire corner into several pieces. For this action, there was indeed an opposite reaction as our guest dramatized his lesson and seemed satisfied with his own fervor. The class was impressed; I was distressed. I explained this "accident" as all in the name of science, but it was nearly two months before I was given a chance to forget the incident. It's quite understandable that adolescents, on occasion, enjoy the demise of the teacher, and I was not the happy camper. Professor Young, our guest, did his best to accommodate the class as his daughter sat in close proximity, horrified and embarrassed at her father's display of ingenuity. How does a teacher thank this parent and at the same time feel some sort of displeasure? Not quite the state of nirvana, yet those traits of patience, composure, humor, and self-control must be eminently visible and apparent for all to see.

Classroom discussions about drugs, alcohol, and tobacco are fascinating, informative, revealing, and valuable. Dr. Smith was a chief thoracic surgeon who consented to talk with my students about the hazards of smoking tobacco. Organizing such an event was time consuming and the logistics required exact timing. To alter students' schedules is forever complex, but the trade-offs are obviously rewarding . . . or so I like to believe.

Dr. Smith was scheduled to arrive at 10:00 A.M. and naturally yours truly, *semper paratus*, as one hundred plus students, several teachers, and some guests, anticipated an imminent arrival as the clock displayed 10:00. At 10:30, no doctor and one hundred plus bodies squirming and chafing as all eyes were directed toward me! Can you picture the scene? Now the ever-present problem of schedule tampering looms as monumental. At 10:50, Dr. Smith finally greeted me at the school entrance. I had almost abandoned this nearly out-of-control, chaotic assemblage to have AT&T come to the rescue; however, the good doctor made his appearance—a presence I liken to the coming of the Messiah.

As we make the beeline to the classroom, Dr. Smith was apologizing (profusely, to the point of my embarrassment) for taking so much time completing another emergency lung operation on a smoker. I pleaded with Dr. Smith to relay some of the details regarding this experience to the students.

As the lecture/demonstration unfolded, an unusual silence was evident, especially in contrast to the pre-doctor presence. This man, whose physical stature was rather small and slight, took control within a few minutes. His quiet, calm demeanor seemed to command a respect and his intelligence was indeed obvious.

I witnessed how the "wise," usually verbose students acquiesced to the questions and suggestions put before them. There were facts and statistics; there were lung specimens from the healthy and the unhealthy: the informative aspect. The "smokers" in the audience volunteered information that normally would not have surfaced: the valuable aspect. Dr. Smith left the specimens and slides with me for future reference and to show other classes.

One time, I was asked to teach or at least conduct a class on careers. This was more like an activity that convened once or twice per week, and there were no grade requirements. I believed that to invite "people with careers" to speak with students and allow for discussions would make this class come alive. Initially, I drew from the class pool, that is, parents and guardians of the students in the class. I would call, brief the prospective guest, and arrange for the visit. Then, after exhausting the parental/guardian approach, I resorted to more general (re)sources. Inevitably, our class was entertained by talented people employed in many varied professions, such as managers of beauty salons, department stores, dress shops, and cosmetic companies, firemen, police officers, doctors, dentists, veterinarians, computer programmers, newspaper editors, bakers, chefs, television producers, teachers, athletes, and a hospital administrator, plus others too numerous to mention. Often these visitors would bring some gadget or appropriate souvenir for class members or perform a demonstration with visual aids.

This class received an excellent rating from my students and, at times, I was made to feel as though my own science classes were superfluous! There was, however, no resentment on my part because I, too, looked forward to these sessions. What had begun as a minor activity turned into a major learning experience for both student and teacher. Another situation where I learned from my students! It was fascinating to hear adolescents ask our visitors questions about their personal lives, and that they did, more so than about their professional life.

What sort of education was necessary? How did you get started? Was it necessary to travel significant distances? Did you pursue the profession you studied for? If not, why not? What was tops on the list that motivated you? Did you have role models? Who were they? Did you have the support of your parents? How long (hours) do you work each week? Is your work hazardous? What, if any, risks are involved?

Suddenly, to my amazement, the questions turned to "benefits." In every instance, students were seriously concerned about compensation. This word was the common denominator, the thread that ran through every discussion. Humorous, embarrassing, serious, playful, sincere, trite: a gamut of emotions that zeroed in on *how much money do you make*? Adolescents seem to have license to ask questions like this—no hinting, no innuendo, no insinuations, and no implications; in other words, no hidden agendas. (Another reason why I enjoy the adolescent.) It was simply, *how much money do you make*?

This was one time I was thrilled to be part of the audience and not on the stage! I did try to soften some blows, but adolescents are naively persistent. *How much money do you make*? This question became a creed, the battle cry, the bottom line; *how much money do you make*?

As the guests responded to this query in a rather general format and insufficient as it was, these questions continued to elicit additional prodding as our guests succumbed to students' demands. *How much money do you make* was on the mind and lips of every class member. Is there a late twentieth-century or twenty-first-century message here?

This careers seminar (as I referred to the course) was one of the most practical seminars I was involved with. The real world entered our classroom world and I observed students generating connections and associations, and relationships beginning to form links in a chain, leading to various events or occupations that can only be achieved by means of an education. Hopefully, these youngsters were beginning to understand the value in and importance of studying.

Teaching and coaching supplemental courses is another activity for which the teacher might not be prepared, and might not have realized that he would be called upon to investigate uncharted territory. However, therein lies the excitement, the drama, the hysteria, the inspiration, and the all to the animated life of the teacher. These supplemental courses often allow for a student and teacher to connect. This connection can happen when and where least expected. Teachers should keep open minds and be prepared to *carpe diem* (seize the day)!

"Permanent" materials are becoming obsolete within just nine months, almost as fast as the consumable goods are consumed! I imagine this word *permanent* will soon be eliminated from the jargon of the teacher. We are certainly aware of the finances involved in trying to keep textbooks up to date and in acquiring sufficient materials to meet the requirements of the varied programs for the special needs students who are now attending regular scheduled classes (inclusion). School budgets hopefully keep pace with the needs of the schools and reflect the commitment of the community to their school system. Mentioning budgets reminds me of taxpayers spending $40 billion a year on the two million inmates in our prisons. Without further calculations, I would guess we are spending more on prisons than on education! Does this send us a message?

It would be impossible to simplify the entire aspect of curriculum planning because this is a complex process, especially when different plans must be considered for certain students. Earlier, I alluded to the fact that a successful school will try to meet the needs of each individual student and that hopefully each student would see the school environment as a place where he could succeed and feel comfortable as his tenure in the school unfolds.

Trying to provide a curriculum and appropriate teaching methods that meet the needs of individual students is by no means a simple task. On the contrary, this task is the primary goal of most teachers. The teacher has devoted her life to this responsibility and therein lies the art of teaching.

The time is here and now for teachers to be prepared to teach special education students in their regular education classes. Four out of five teachers with special education students in their classes feel ill prepared to teach them. This is being addressed in the colleges; no longer are special education teachers isolated in small classrooms. Many of them (330,000 nationwide) work daily with regular classroom teachers, and district administrators see this as a way of educating future teachers.

Special education is in the limelight as the special needs status of students is being challenged. There are loads of studies on this subject; one study recently suggested that taxpayers could save several ($157) million dollars by cutting 30,000 students from the program. Naturally, any report that seeks to alter mandated special education guidelines will anger and annoy the special education advocates. Many are also concerned with the long-term costs to society. Both sides do agree, however, that communities require additional funds to pay for this education and that teachers need more training. The training is taking place; it's the missing part of the equation—the funding—that is not taking place!

Specifically, that training includes, in part, attending workshops. These workshops make teachers aware of some of the latest strategies and they outline goals, principles, and techniques for "watering up" curriculum and instruction. It is believed that accommodations "water down" the curriculum by reducing opportunities to learn and that those accommodations emphasize memorization of facts. "Watering up the curriculum creates "thought-full" classrooms where there exist a higher order of thinking and information processing skills with more depth and less superficial coverage" (Ellis 1997).

Prior to mainstreaming, there existed not only the special needs students referred to above but a more specific group of youngsters organized in a class for "developmentally delayed." Many schools were fortunate to be able to offer this sort of global disability program and have a trained staff at the helm. This program involved all academics in addition to social aspects, vocabulary and language skills, and daily living skills. The students were taught what to wear, how to act, how to budget their money, and how to shop and prepare meals.

Another tangent to my career was becoming acquainted with these boys and girls. Apparently, my disposition lent itself (so I was told) to working with Sandra and Ken in the homeroom setting only. Both of them helped make my mornings! They certainly afforded me an opportunity to begin my day on a positive note. These two always arrived with a smile, never complained, always were respectful, always willing to assist me; and at that price, how could one refuse such help? Teachers! Accept all the assistance that comes your way; you will never regret it. How many employers receive this sort of benefit from their employees each (and every) morning? If there exists one or two, I would like to shake their hand!

The longer I live, the more I experience people who have much to complain about, yet do the least complaining. Sandra and Ken did not belong to the Girl Scouts or Boy Scouts, but they definitely exemplified the motto of the organizations.

I would often visit their classroom and become involved with their lessons, especially when academics came into play. At times, I would bring them a film dealing with a science topic or present a demonstration. Their interest and willingness to learn impressed me to the point of asking, "When can I return?"

Be patient: the following is neither a harangue on retirement nor more on curriculum, simply an experience that will forever remain in my memory.

There are several people and a few organizations that usually wish to acknowledge the retiring teacher. A few features of this recognition involve speeches, accolades for better or worse, reminiscing (now that's retirement), and of course, the "rest of the party"! No doubt, these recollections demonstrate an appreciation for a colleague's dedication and commitment. One such party that meant the most to me.

A few youngsters with their teachers planned a surprise festive occasion for yours truly. What impressed me most was their genuine thoughtfulness and desire for me to enjoy myself. These young people made the cake and the cookies, gave the speeches, and made my day and my final year. These kids and their teachers deserved the tribute, but I admit I was as excited as my grandson is now when attending a birthday party.

For me, a panacea is meeting the needs of every student in a regular classroom, a classroom with an enrollment of ten to twelve students (maximum), a classroom where all teachers are trained in all aspects of education ("regular" and "special"), including tracking process and evaluating the ongoing progress of every student.

Every teacher's goal is to help all students be the best they can be. To be sure, this is indeed an honorable goal, yet these goals cannot be realized by every student no matter how hard the teacher tries. It is, however, important to have goals in place; professionals use goals as guidelines as they pursue these ambitions.

This is another perspective for teachers to consider as they prepare for their exciting journey. Notice I mentioned the word *prepare*. Preparation is vital because (in this example) 8 percent of the special education teaching force is improperly certified to work with disabled students, and among general teachers, the preparedness is worse—an additional example of how the teacher's life is synonymous with perpetual studying and learning.

Observing a teacher in action is similar to the unveiling of a work of art. Where the artist tries to capture a mood or a moment with color and possibly an expression, so does the teacher try to captivate an audience and elicit a response with words, actions, and expressions. The interactions, the innuendoes, the intonations, and the expressions along with the variations in pitch emanating from the class parallel the feelings and emotions elicited from the viewing of this "masterpiece." This art is at the core of our educational existence. Teaching is a talent with the techniques, training, dialogue, technology, and subtleties all adding up to a form of art. Who was the critic who said, "Beauty is in the eye of the beholder!"

Well, my TLC is the Teaching, Learning, and Cultivating of both student and teacher. *Reality 101: To Be a Teacher and Teach, Too* is not intended to make light of serious important matters but rather to present a different perspective on the trials and the tribulations of the teacher.

My purpose in this book is to emphasize, with specifics, that there exists so much more to "being" a teacher than most people or even the beginning teacher realizes; that so much teaching and learning occurs out-side the classroom; that many professionals play a part in the educa-tional process of teacher and student; that the classroom occupies a small fraction of the total educational environment; and that it is this to-tal "playing field" that must be considered.

I hope I have presented a variety of alternative scenarios to aid in maintaining a semblance of sanity for a teacher and presented some in-sights into ways of looking at teaching as a career. Sometimes, it's good to step off the merry-go-round, step back, take a deep breath, and observe.

As teachers use their ingenuity, listen, are patient, loving, kind, and considerate, they will learn on a daily basis. They *will be* effective as teachers and role models and will affect the lives of the people they choose to influence and educate!

I certainly have not, nor could I, touch all the bases in the plant; how-ever, I want to point out specifically that there are definite areas that beckon or require the assistance of the teacher regardless of the teacher's training or expertise—sort of "fringe benefits" that are in-cluded (unwritten) in the contract.

Once upon a time, I asked myself, "Why am I monitoring this john (or this corridor, or the cafeteria)? No teacher takes pleasure observing ado-lescents devour food. "Why am I climbing this mountain" with young-sters in the midst of a snowstorm (that really happened!) bringing up the rear, only to arrive at a hut (minus any heat source) where four of these "campers" had already staked out their territory and yours truly, once again, was awarded the last pickings?

"Why am I monitoring this busload of students" on a field trip? A trip that many teachers prefer to eliminate in the first place? "Why am I re-turning to school in the evening?" To watch my students perform in a play or play their instruments in the band or orchestra. My added trav-eling time was an hour plus, so why did I leave for home in the first place? Maybe to remind my own family that I still reside with them. "Why am I calling these (some) parents in the evening?" Some of whom even ask me who I am.

I cannot be answering my rhetorical questions with dollar signs! I must be responding with other compensatory benefits, one of which is because I'm the teacher who is responsible for the educating, the nur-turing, and the cultivating of the students in and out of the classroom.

This, I believe, is the life of the teacher, the students' school life. Sprinkle some patience and understanding, add a dash of love, mix this with your energy, and in the correct proportions—and both student and teacher will have a successful career.

CONCLUSIONS

Amidst all antagonists, the teacher looms as a superhuman who is required to assist with a myriad of responsibilities. These responsibilities may or may not have a direct bearing on teaching, and many people believe these additional responsibilities go with the territory of teaching. Some responsibilities demand additional training and some not; however, those activities that do demand more training involve time and energy in order to be incorporated into the teacher's tight schedule.

In Massachusetts, the governor's office and the Department of Education are now working on guidelines for teaching character. Here we go again: drawing up guidelines to address responsibility and tolerance. I assume these traits are included in character awareness, and I also assume time will be allotted for the energy to work on this. I believe, in spite of the teacher bashing, that good citizenship, responsibility, tolerance, and character are routinely spelled out throughout the school day. Are individual guidelines really necessary, or is this another political ploy?

We have safety experts explaining the need for tightening up security, especially in light of school violence across our country. Important, yes indeed; time consuming, yes indeed; however, we must be aware of the fact that teachers will need some training as these programs unfold. I mention programs (plural) because as the schools are called upon to deal with antiviolence programs, there must be an awareness of child-abuse programs and suicide-prevention programs—both of which are already also addressed by many a faculty.

During my career, I found it very difficult to teach my subject matter (math and science) *and* at the same time include some "of society's ills" into the curriculum; it can be accomplished, but only with time, patience, and planning.

I volunteered to teach alcohol education and underwent extensive training. One objective of the city was to have a comprehensive syllabus or manual produced that would include ideas and suggestions for teachers of several grade levels in all schools to use, and this was accomplished with the help of some summer study. Of course, as the materials were tried and tested, teachers could revamp the materials to suit individual situations.

I decided to insert some of the factual materials into lessons dealing with the human body and how this remarkable machine processes alcohol from entry to elimination. Naturally, several other issues surfaced and as one could imagine we (yours truly and class) entertained some fascinating and delicate dialogue. Certainly, guest speakers, audio-visual aids, and relevant up-to-date materials were put into use. I did my best to create a comfortable atmosphere where any student could state an opinion or relate a personal experience. In the end, I was quite satisfied with the way the lessons were accepted and the manner in which the students conducted themselves. No preaching, no moral judgments, no value judgments, just good honest down-to-earth discussions. To this day, I hope these discussions benefited many students and provided them with positive feelings, and I certainly hope they went away with some basic information to make informed decisions.

At this time, I wish to add that I also volunteered to become involved in the school's drug education program—that is, to work with others to organize a definite program with much material. To this end, four educators from the city (Newton, Massachusetts) worked endlessly to put together a kit, much the same as I did for the alcohol education program, only more comprehensive. The "we" consisted of a representative from our education center, one teacher from each of the high schools, and me representing the middle schools (at the time, five junior high schools). We gathered several of the most up-to-date materials, including books written by recognized experts in the field, and put these in boxes to be distributed to all of the Newton schools.

Much training had been required to examine several reports and journals and to meet with addicts and many people from the medical community. Fascinating experiences for me, to be sure, and what a great opportunity to help others. If we could make some inroads in the lives of these young people at this time of their lives, we would consider ourselves fortunate to have had the opportunity to influence or inform.

To include another example of an addition to the curriculum that addressed a significant "health problem," I committed our science department to a five-year unit from the American Cancer Society on antismoking! We satisfied the requirements for this duration and then had license to either abandon or keep the unit. I chose to do a combination of both acceptance and rejection. Segments of this topic were inserted into our studies of the respiratory, circulatory, and nervous systems. Of course, other pieces of this unit entailed adding visitors (e.g., nurses and doctors), slides, tapes, and the ever-present "advertisements." I tried very hard to explain and show how smoking can damage our bodies.

In addition to this, there were several antismoking activities, many sponsored by the county Drug Abuse Resistance Education programs. There are also board of health collaborators who come to present talks and discussions to preteens and teenagers.

Situations such as these would be beautiful opportunities for students to relay their "before" and "after" feelings following exposure to these topics; I took advantage of this in class! What great material for student essays.

I wish to include another slant on testing, creativity, grade-point averages, and how states would work with this. Dr. Thomas Stanley states in his book *The Millionaire Mind* "that our economy is filled with successful entrepreneurs who were encouraged early in their lives to think differently—creativity was nurtured."

Many educators focus only on the part of the brain that houses analytical intellect. "If kids are told test scores are inferior, therefore you're inferior; we are in trouble. . . . Tell kids . . . social skills, common sense, and integrity make for productive citizens. Testing has its place, but we need more testing of interests kids have—how well one does involves much more than grade-point averages."

During my years in teaching, I have witnessed a breakdown of the home and the public perception of the role of the teacher. In 1972, 73 percent of children lived with their original parents, the latest figure is 52 percent. This fact alone has added a tremendous burden on the school and the teachers.

The 2000 census shows that more than 2.4 million grandparents have their grandchildren living with them and have a significant role in caring for those children. According to Amy Goyer, coordinator of the AARP Grandparent Information Center, "more grandparents are shouldering the responsibilities of parents." Remember one of my scenarios in chapter 14? During the past decade, the number of children living with grandparents (now at 4.5 million) increased 30 percent, even though the total number of children under 18 increased by only 14.3 percent.

Add this to the lack of pride and commitment on the part of some students, in addition to a vast array of psychological problems, and we could have a generation of youth breeding contempt, disaster, continued violence, lack of manners, and a total disrespect for any form of authority. This behavior becomes contagious and spreads like a cancer; it must be treated in its early stages to become effective and affect the generation.

The reality check is that these students are in the minority yet they consume a majority of the teachers' time. These students require special attention and many receive it. The public school does more than its share of providing much assistance to enable the students with a sundry of problems to attend classes with the least amount of stress (for student *and* teacher)! The teacher must and will learn to deal with the problematic student and his family. Remember, I did refer earlier to the assistance afforded the teacher working in these situations. Recently, I wrote an article to one of our local newspapers regarding teacher training. I cited as a major priority that teachers need mentors and must continue to serve internships, similar to other professionals. Teachers obviously require supervision and support to achieve a degree of proficiency as committed professionals.

I was fortunate to have worked with mentors and a patient community that realized (and still does) that education was their #1 commodity. This community was willing and able to support the educational process and thereby reap the rewards.

Active communities take advantage of programs through special funding, such as a program that will offer training for parents in antiracist terminology and other programs for students to learn about antiracist practices and respect for human differences.

An article in the *Boston Globe* (September 26, 1999) mentioned that, given a choice of ways to improve schools (from a previous Harris poll), the respondents ranked "providing a qualified teacher in every classroom" as far more important than the fashionable political solutions, such as state-imposed tests, vouchers, and uniforms.

We now have Jack Valenti, chairman and CEO of the Motion Picture Association, proposing a nationwide ethics course for students in preschool through about the fifth grade to counter violence in society. After reading Steve Allen's book *Vulgarians at the Gate*, I understand that Mr. Valenti is not only a paid spokesman and lobbyist for the entertainment industry, he is also a former member of the advisory board of the Parents Television Council. How Mr. Valenti can propose and be a spokesperson while violence and sex permeate the motion picture industry is something I cannot fathom. I realize the major studios do not produce "all" the movies; however, they do produce (a few) too many! This is certainly hypocritical and indeed disappointing, because these people have the power to contribute so much, yet choose to ignore their influence. I agree that Mr. Valenti is sincere in his endeavors, yet he must exert a more consistent and intensive effort to combat "the sleaze merchants now so dominant in the entertainment professions." We sure do expect the teacher to set an example and it is certainly a monumental task fighting these uphill battles. There are too many distractions for the schools to do it all and maintain order!

Massachusetts is now taking an initiative in preventing school violence. The Massachusetts Youth Violence Summit includes students, law enforcement personnel, religious and school leaders, parents, and community people. It is just one of many efforts to help maintain a safe educational environment.

Overcrowding is another major issue in the schools. Enrollment in many school districts is increasing and only now are new schools under construction to accommodate these increases. Unfortunately, predicted enrollments will outpace what is on the drawing boards. Therefore, more schools are needed and more space is needed in many existing schools. Oh, what teachers could do with more spacious classrooms! Tell this to the teacher or assistant who might share quarters that resemble a closet rather than a classroom. Let's hope the citizens are as patient with the teachers as they purport to be with their elected officials living through this state of flux.

Schools are or will be called upon to work closely with various hospitals and departments of public health. Forums will be presented to parents and educators to help identify those students requiring such services. This multipronged approach is needed. These mental health services will be put into place in addition to a plan of how schools will respond to potential disasters and no longer only fire drills. In other words, much work must be accomplished to assist communities in creating a safe, sound environment. To reiterate: *semper paratus* (always a smart move)!

I recently read an article entitled "More Schools Becoming Mental Health Clinics." There are school-based mental health advocates in schools who believe kids are being abused, neglected, violent, or depressed. Therefore, Dr. Weist, a therapist and director of the Center for School Mental Health Assistance at the University of Maryland, expects child psychologists, school health professionals, health educators, family members, legislators, and teachers to devise ways of improving mental health care in schools. I do hope the teachers saved those Psychology 101 notes and at least had a minor in psychology! Here we go again and again and again: the schools are given additional responsibilities in their approach to serving the best possible interests of their students. The latter part of this statement is a given; it's the former aspect of the statement that conjures up panic! Will training be provided? By whom? When? Will proper time be devoted? Where in the program will it be inserted? What type of program? Will evaluations be built in? Are these evaluations necessary? Will the program be monitored? Will parents and others be notified of plans?

By now, it becomes obvious that so much more is expected of the teacher than even the teacher realizes. It's not enough to state, "the added responsibilities come with the territory," as I mentioned earlier.

Putting it that way trivializes the significance of the tasks and the urgency of hiring and retaining qualified teachers.

The teacher is not simply confined to the classroom. The teacher automatically becomes part of a community. The teacher inherently becomes involved with the lives of many families. This involvement takes on many characteristics; some are humorous, some not so humorous, while others are indeed serious and sad. However, throughout all these contacts, the teacher must be that other superhuman with the patience of Job, the love of a mother, and the understanding, humility, empathy, and wisdom of Lao-tse!

The teacher must be imbued with these characteristics to be a partner in these endeavors, and no teacher test can measure such attributes. I believe that compassion should be first and foremost—that is, revealing a *mensch*, and then the remainder of the teaching skills will fall into place as the internship, monitoring, and guidance processes take hold.

The bottom line should read that teaching is not simply imparting information, but rather involving the interaction of many complex feelings, ideas, and relationships. Put this all together with the "additional" responsibilities and the teacher's role becomes monumental. So often we have heard conversations about other professionals that are brilliant, adept, and conscientious as far as knowledge of their craft is concerned, yet would receive a failing grade for bedside manners. Sound familiar? Well, can you imagine this same scenario when referring to teachers? To be sure, the doctor "treats," teaching becomes secondary, yet the teacher must teach and treat every student. Once, twice, again, I wish to point out that this teacher is expected to be everything to everyone. A dedicated teacher will do just that and more!

Certainly, my intent is not to convey messages of strife within the schools. In fact, the schools are dominated by honorable, serious, kind, and considerate people, many of whom do not (unfortunately) make the headlines but who do make their schools and family proud of them.

This issue is another of my pet peeves. The news (media) should be inundated with and feature the lives of the "contributors" in our schools. Similar to a TV show (that does not exist) depicting the "responsible." In other words, those people who are dedicated and committed to a cause (marriage, employment, volunteer, or recreation) as they try their best to make a difference and influence the lives of others.

Teachers! Do not listen to those who see fit to ridicule and demean the profession. As bashing of public education continues, pay heed to the Paul Newmans and Ben Cohens who speak for Business Leaders for Sensible Priorities. This organization is well aware of our country's shortcomings in money spent on education. They know that the United States ranks #1 in the world in military spending and #10 in per student spending on education. This group, according to the National Education Association, is now launching a massive media campaign that calls for the reallocation of federal funds from the Pentagon to domestic programs in education.

Even in the early 1800s, John Adams emphatically urged the widest possible support for education. "Laws for the liberal education of youth, especially for the lower classes of people, are so extremely wise and useful that to a humane and generous mind, no expense for this purpose would be thought extravagant.

Did anyone notice that there was not much mention of teacher remuneration until now? I'm referring specifically to money for the teachers' salaries. I do apologize for this earlier (intentional) omission because the reader might assume the dedication is lost if such terminology as the word *money* is mentioned. In many circles, the teacher who dares mention the like is deemed unprofessional. What a carryover from the 50s mentality! Let's add respect; let's put the teacher on the pedestal with other professionals, and let's allow the nonteachers in on the life of the teacher. Hopefully, this manuscript touched some soft *and* some hard spots, enlightening many and presenting a different perspective to the people who use the schools for target practice!

Many times we ask ourselves how can our society improve our schools. What is it that makes some schools work better than others? Well, there are the schools on military bases run by the Department of Defense that have a better record than most public schools in this country, according to an article written by Daniel Golden in the *Wall Street Journal* (December 1999). Actually, Mr. Anthony Lewis (*New York Times* News Service) wrote about this, based on the *Journal's* article. Mr. Lewis states that some of the practices that help account for the good showing of the base schools could readily be duplicated in ordinary public schools. The article did mention a few specific factors, such as spending more money on schools, parent involvement, and stringent discipline policy. There is no hint of a militarized system, simply a suggestion that we should be able to learn from their successes.

Each and every event, encounter, or scenario presents its own message. Most situations were pleasant, some unpleasant, and a very few intolerable (revealing in itself). Unabridged, they are intended to relate some of the intricacies, treasures, and just plain life in the society in and about the school.

I believe the very simplicity of many scenarios paints a clear picture of the responsibilities bestowed upon a teacher. I thrived on my teaching in spite of the lack of sufficient rest. I ran, walked, jumped, skipped, and even backpedaled. I just about ate, drank, and thought about school twenty or more hours each day. I also experienced anger, frustration, disappointment, and frequently joy in Teacherville!

I taught through the times of the Civil Rights march and the John F. Kennedy assassination, from apathy and conformity to the wave of idealism and feelings of commitment, Lyndon Johnson's social improvement including the great "educational bill," the Civil Rights bill, antipoverty projects, and a war. Following the death of John F. Kennedy, love was a dominant mood; remember the Beatles— "All You Need Is Love." I lived through a deterioration of society's faith in public education. We were witnessing violence and the continued use of illicit drugs in the schools. Manners, respect for others, and personal property were becoming nonexistent. The taxpayer viewed her bill on the rise, a substantial portion of which was earmarked for the schools, and this conjured up a problem! What are the schools doing with the additional funds? Shouldn't the schools be improving? Shouldn't we see a more humane side of these young men and women? A negative perception of the value of education persisted. President Reagan tried to spell out his goals, yet several of the reforms failed.

President Bush appropriated $250+ million for programs in the schools, and I understand the use of alcohol and drugs declined. At least the educational systems in our country were drawing more attention.

The National Commission on Excellence in Education (NCEE) published their "infamous" report, "A Nation at Risk." In part, this report stated "it was imperative that our educational system develop talents of all students to the fullest extent." We teachers were devoting our energies to this principle on several fronts long before the commission's report went to print. With our public education system in flux and our backs to the wall, we have choices remaining—choices we are now exercising.

Educate our prospective teachers with sound subject matter background, excellent supervision throughout those early teaching years, and sufficient funding.

All of the above will allow teachers to detect, intervene, and possibly prevent problems, and (the Lord knows), *even teach*.

Educational and economic opportunities did improve. Moon landings made the headlines as did computers (calculating millions of times faster than the brain), lasers, and the work deciphering genetic codes.

There really is no ending to this "learned discussion." To prepare to teach, to practice teaching, to enjoy teaching, means to live a life of teaching and learning. I still believe we would all be much better served if we "tested" prospective teachers for character—that is, what sort of a person is this teacher? This theory is much more aptly described in the Talmud: "Everything depends upon the sort of a person a man is." The question now becomes, how do we test for this?

I suppose I am concluding this book with similar feelings and impressions about teachers and teaching as I began this book, especially when I refer to teacher characteristics and qualifications. Can you believe these theories have not changed during the course of this writing?

The teacher is the battery that allows the auto engine to start, the seed that enables the flowers to grow and blossom; the teacher is the foundation of the building that allows for superstructures to be built, and this teacher is the heart that enables the blood to permeate the active body and spirit.

To emphasize further, I have observed (possibly) the best-prepared teaching candidates—candidates, that is, who have received extensive training and preparation in methodology. However, I witnessed in these same teachers a lack of the very characteristics that I deemed vital for "successful" teaching. I honestly believe these teachers were excellent with the "mechanics" of teaching, yet quite limited in the dynamics of relating to youngsters. Through no fault of their own, these teachers were not blessed with the intangibles that I believe are necessary to be successful. These teachers will pass (or have already passed) their certification exams with flying colors, but such certification does not determine whether or not a person will be a good teacher. I hope the staunch supporters of such certification tests will stand tall and realize the flip side of the coin.

I also believe there are two important questions that need be asked, one question asked of the candidate, the other *by* the candidate, both *for* the candidate.

Why do *you* want to teach?

Why do I want to teach?

Professor Elie Wiesel said, "To witness the awakening of knowledge, that unique light of understanding, of recognition—is there a more beautiful moment for a teacher?" As an addendum to teacher training, Massachusetts has formally adopted (into state licensing regulations) its two-year-old Massachusetts Institute for New Teachers program. Similar to programs offered in various other states, this is an effort to get midcareer professionals into teaching. Those candidates accepted must take a seven-week summer course and then are given professional certification. This certification will allow them to begin their teaching in the fall (beginning in October 2001).

I cannot imagine a crash course coming to the rescue! I cannot imagine a balancing act between content material and teaching skills in such short term! More time should be allotted to the planning and the implementing of such a (drastic) program. I find it difficult to understand that as we try to increase student proficiency in various studies, at the same time we begin to offer a quick-fix solution for an improved educational stance by hiring teachers who will have been exposed to such minimal preparation!

I hope our country takes notice, because I begin to see how lack of thought and adequate planning can convert impatience to panic. In light of these crash programs that are immediate-needs-based throughout our country, I observe a stifling and abandonment of creative, inventive, and productive programs.

Changes and alterations in this process of education must come slowly, sort of a walk before a run. If educators' primary goal is to hurry through a planned curriculum without regard for current, pertinent history, our country will realize diminishing returns.

I am reminded of the early '60s when, for the first time, our country began to administer Jonas Salk's polio vaccine. Mass immunization was taking place before our eyes. After receiving the vaccine, students returned to their classrooms, prompting me to ask my students if they were aware that "history was in the making today."

We were required to follow a curriculum, yet what a great opportunity to launch our study of immunity. Indeed, this was a detour from the subject matter in process, yet to surrender such an opportunity would have been a crime—at least, to my way of thinking.

Analogous to this scenario would be for teachers to seize the opportunities that abound regarding the 2000 presidential election saga. I would hope that teachers would see fit to delve into this "history in the making" in spite of the necessity to follow set curriculum.

A final comfort zone: Teachers are blessed with what I call a "recovery system." Lessons will go awry, mistakes will be made, and plans will actually fall apart. All this can lead to disaster for students and teachers. Yet in spite of this, "tomorrow is another day": a day to correct what went wrong.

Lest I forget to complete "that" decision from the earlier chapter. . . . We did allow our son to drive that night, had faith in his good judgment, and all was well that ends well.

BIBLIOGRAPHY

Albom, Mitch. *Tuesdays with Morrie*. New York: Doubleday, 1997.

Allen, Steve. *Vulgarians at the Gate*. New York: Prometheus Books, 2001.

Bondi, Victor, ed. *American Decades 1980–1989*. Detroit: Gale Research, 1996.

Carlson, Richard. *Don't Sweat the Small Stuff—And It's All Small Stuff: Simple Ways to Keep the Little Things from Taking Over Your Life*. New York: Hyperion, 1997.

Ellis, Edwin. "Watering Up the Curriculum for Adolescents with Learning Disabilities." *Remedial and Special Education Abstracts* 18, no. 6 (November/December 1997): 326–46.

———. "Watering Up the Curriculum for Adolescents with Learning Disabilities." *Remedial and Special Education Abstracts* 19, no. 2 (March/April 1998): 91–105.

Evaluation Handbook. Newton, Mass.: Office of Human Resources, Newton Public Schools, 1998.

Hine, Thomas. *The Rise and Fall of the American Teenager*. New York: Bard, 1999.

Kronholz, June. "Senate Passes Education Bill in Victory for Bush," *Wall Street Journal*, 19 December 2001.

Lewis, Thomas. *The Lives of a Cell: Notes of a Biology Watcher*. New York: Viking, 1974.

McCullough, David. *John Adams*. New York: Simon & Schuster, 2001.

Root-Bernstein, Robert, and Michèle Root-Bernstein. *Sparks of Genius*. Boston: Houghton Mifflin, 1999.

Rothstein, Richard. "The Education Bill: Many Trials Ahead," *New York Times*, 19 December 2001.

Schemo, Diane Jean. "Senate Approves a Bill to Expand the Federal Role in Public Education," *New York Times*, 19 December 2001.

Siegal, Bernie. *Prescriptions for Living: Inspirational Lessons for a Joyful, Loving Life*. New York: Harper Collins, 1998.

Stanley, Thomas. *The Millionaire Mind*. Kansas City, Mo.: Andrews McMeel, 2000.

Students' Rights and Responsibilities: A Handbook. Newton, Mass.: Newton Public Schools, 1998.

This Fabulous Century, 1950–1960. Vol. 6. Alexandria, Va.: Time-Life Books, 1985.

This Fabulous Century, 1960–1970. Vol. 7. Alexandria, Va.: Time-Life Books, 1985.

Wiesel, Elie. *And the Sea Is Never Full: Memoirs 1969*. Trans. Marion Wiesel. New York: Knopf, 1999.

Zlotowitz, Meir, and Nosson Scherman. *Ethics of the Fathers*. Brooklyn, N.Y.: Mesorah Publications, 1984.

ABOUT THE AUTHOR

Milton E. Rosenthal received his B.A. and M.A. degrees in science from Boston University and attended the Harvard University Graduate Teaching/Newton Summer program in mathematics. He began his professional life as a research assistant, working on a U.S. Public Health Service Grant at Boston University Biological Research Laboratories, and spent the next forty years teaching math and science in the Newton, Massachusetts, public schools.

He has designed and implemented curricula for alcohol and drug education, black studies, advanced challenge and vocational education. He also has had articles on "original" experiments adapted (with permission from research) for middle/high school students published in *The Science Teacher*, the journal of the National Science Teachers Association.

Mr. Rosenthal received a regional award for writing materials on the understanding of other peoples and other cultures: science/religion (an interest derived from his teaching of religious school). He received the STAR Award (Science Teaching Achievement Recognition), the outstanding teacher award from his school in 1997, and is also included in the first edition (1990) of *Who's Who among America's*

Teachers. Most recently, he was to be included in the 21st century edition of *Who's Who in America*.

This year, he and his wife will celebrate their fortieth wedding anniversary. They have two children and two grandchildren. They currently reside in Randolph, Massachusetts.